GEORGE COCHRAN LAMBDIN

GEORGE COCHRAN LAMBDIN
1830–1896

Essay by RUTH IRWIN WEIDNER

The Exhibition

September 6 through November 23, 1986

BRANDYWINE RIVER MUSEUM

Chadds Ford, Pennsylvania

This publication and exhibition have been made
possible by a grant from The Mabel Pew Myrin Trust.

COVER: 18 IN THE GREENHOUSE, n.d. (detail)
Courtesy of The Metropolitan Museum of Art,
gift of Mrs. J. Augustus Barnard

FRONTISPIECE: Cat. J. George Cochran Lambdin in his studio.
Courtesy of the Historical Society of Pennsylvania

PREFACE

The first work by George Cochran Lambdin to hang in the Brandywine River Museum was a single painting, "The Dead Wife," part of a special exhibition in 1981. That painting held the attention of everyone visiting the exhibition and it led the Museum staff to search for Lambdin's work from that time forward. We came to know him especially as a painter of still lifes, wonderful floral subjects, and to recognize qualities unique to his work. Several of his paintings were included in an exhibition of flowers in American art organized by Gėnė E. Harris in 1984. To a large extent, our enthusiasm for Lambdin relates to this Museum's dedication to American still life painting and our fine collection of such work. Our further interest derives from the artist's origins in the Delaware Valley. Thus, for several years we hoped to organize an exhibition devoted entirely to George Cochran Lambdin. No such effort has been mounted since his death; it is long overdue.

Ruth Irwin Weidner, Associate Professor of Art History at West Chester University, has made this exhibition possible. She has had a long-standing dedication to the artist, and both this publication and the exhibition it represents result from her years of research and writing. We delight, as she does, in her discovery of many works included in the exhibition as the result of diligent research. Here are three of Lambdin's rare and thought provoking Civil War subjects; many of his little-known and delightful genre works, which when seen side by side, teach us about his stylistic development and European influences; and of course, here is a profusion of the beautiful floral paintings for which he is best known and which prove him a master in the representation of roses and other blossoms.

If Lambdin excellently presented his floral subjects, Professor Weidner comprehensively presents Lambdin's life and career in her essay. Her scholarship will allow others to become more familiar with this artist who should gain wider recognition for contributions to American art history, and we are grateful to Ruth Irwin Weidner for her personal contribution to that end. We are also grateful to the many generous lenders and to the Mabel Pew Myrin Trust for its supporting grant. They have made this endeavor possible.

James H. Duff, *Director*
Brandywine River Museum

5

ACKNOWLEDGMENTS

The following persons kindly shared information or expedited research and loans: Henry Adams, Kenneth L. Ames, Amanda Austin, Frank K. Bjornsgaard, Annette Blaugrund, Ann Barton Brown, Russell E. Burke III, Bernadette Callery, Karin Calvert, Gerald S. Dobbs, James Duffin, Kenneth Finkel, Abigail Booth Gerdts, Morris Goldsmith, Audrey Hall, J. Malcolm Henderson, Sinclair H. Hitchings, Lisabeth M. Holloway, Barbara Ickes, Bob Kahler, Cheryl Leibold, Kenneth Lux, John G. Martin, Kathy Martinez, Andrea Pethö, Karen Phillips, Kathleen Reed, Melinda S. Scanlon, Robert Schlatter, Robert D. Schwarz, Linda Stanley, Katherine Stewart, Catherine Stover, Mary Sweeney, Suzanne Thorin, Michele Wolfe, and David Wooters. I have drawn heavily on the resources of the following libraries, and I thank their staff members: Historical Society of Pennsylvania; Library Company of Philadelphia; Library of Congress; National Museum of American Art and Archives of American Art; Pennsylvania Academy of Fine Arts; University of Delaware; Winterthur Museum.

This study began in 1982 at University of Delaware, Department of Art History, in a graduate seminar directed by Visiting Professor John Wilmerding. I should like to acknowledge my indebtedness to Dr. Wilmerding for his role in the project's genesis and for the ideas and insights offered by his teaching.

It has been a very great pleasure to develop this exhibition in conjunction with the Brandywine River Museum. I have enjoyed my associations with its staff and thank them, especially James H. Duff, Director, Gènè Harris, Curator of Collections, and Virginia A. Herrick, Assistant Curator.

Most especially, I should like to thank my children, Donna Weidner, David Weidner, and Margaret Weidner, for information from their various fields of expertise and for the assistance which has lightened and enlivened my work. I am grateful to Margaret, a competent bibliographer in the humanities, for working with me at a crucial stage in the research.

Ruth Irwin Weidner
Guest Curator

We are deeply indebted to the many generous individuals and institutions who graciously agreed to lend to this exhibition, including The Academy of Natural Sciences of Philadelphia; The Arden Collection; Artemis Gallery; Mr. and Mrs. Robert Austin; Berry-Hill Galleries; Board of Governors of the Federal Reserve System; Chester County Historical Society; Harry and Fern Cohen; Dr. and Mrs. David Edelbaum; Elvehjem Museum of Art, University of Wisconsin; Mr. and Mrs. Richard M. Flynn; Henry Melville Fuller; John H. Garzoli Fine Art; George Walter Vincent Smith Art Museum; Germantown Historical Society; Hamilton College Library; Historical Society of Pennsylvania; The Hunt Institute of Botanical Documentation, Carnegie-Mellon University; Indianapolis Museum of Art; Kennedy Galleries; Library of Congress; R.H. Love Galleries, Inc.; Mr. and Mrs. Jack Marino; The Metropolitan Museum of Art; Museum of Fine Arts, St. Petersburg, Florida; Moore Collection, Courtesy R.H. Love Galleries, Inc.; Dr. Boyd Myers; National Academy of Design Archives; National Museum of American Art, Smithsonian Institution; The National Trust for Historic Preservation; New York State Historical Association; North Carolina Museum of Art; The Pennsylvania Academy of the Fine Arts Archives; Mr. and Mrs. Walter Rubin; St. Johnsbury Athenaeum; Frank S. Schwarz and Son; M.R. Schweitzer, Schweitzer Gallery; Mr. and Mrs. Charles Shoemaker, Courtesy of Charles B. Taylor, Los Angeles, and Richard York Gallery, New York; J.M. Smucker Company; Ms. Alexandra Steele; Mr. and Mrs. Richard Trotter; Lagakos Turak Gallery; Special Collections, Van Pelt Library, University of Pennsylvania; University of Delaware Library; Washington County Museum of Fine Arts; Whistler Gallery, Inc.; Mr. and Mrs. George C. Woodward; Yale University Art Gallery, and to those anonymous lenders who helped make this exhibition a success.

Ruth Irwin Weidner,
Guest Curator
Gènè E. Harris
Curator of Collections

1 GIRL IN A LAVENDER DRESS, n.d.
Courtesy of the Museum of Fine Arts, St. Petersburg, Florida

32 MUSIC AND REFRESHMENTS, 1875. *Courtesy of the New York State Historical Association, Cooperstown*

GEORGE COCHRAN LAMBDIN

"Un *Sensitif* d'un ordre exquis"
(Paul Mantz, 1867)[1]

The quiet and serious children, gentle, refined women, softly lit domestic interiors, verdant bowers—and especially the profusion of lush flowers—draw our attention and delight our eyes. Surrounded by these paintings, we are strongly impressed by George Cochran Lambdin's extraordinary understanding of the possibilities and subtleties of color, his remarkable ability to convey the texture of petals, fabrics, and skin tones, and his sure sense of structure and balance in composition. It is easy to understand why this Philadelphia painter (1830–1896) was a great favorite in his own day. And the present exhibition, the first event in one-hundred years to bring together a large number of Lambdin paintings, provides a welcome and timely opportunity to affirm his important place in American art.

A century ago the spotlight of public and critical attention shone brightly on Lambdin, whose reputation was considerable and far-reaching. He was active in Philadelphia and New York artistic circles, he exhibited widely, his works were well reviewed when exhibited and were collected by several leading patrons of the arts, he was well acquainted with other major artists and leading critics of his time, and his flower studies were widely distributed as chromolithographs by the Boston firm of Louis Prang. "Lambdin's roses" were known and loved by many Americans and have secured his place among the best flower painters of all times.

Yet, in the 1890s, Lambdin passed from success and fame into obscurity, and only recently have scholars reintroduced him as a painter whose areas of spe-cialization are of particular interest within American art history.[2] In the very diversity of Lambdin's subject matter may lie a clue to his having escaped from critical attention for so long. His oeuvre includes sentimental and anecdotal genre scenes, studies of young women, Civil War subjects, and the flower still lifes which have brought him such great fame. When one closely examines the seemingly dissimilar categories of his work, one senses that their strongest common thread is Lambdin's own attitude or viewpoint. And this point of view is so characteristically nineteenth century that it is understandable that generations of twentieth century critics, concerned as they were with the staggering artistic developments of our own century, should have considered George Cochran Lambdin *retardataire*. For several generations, as critical favor focused on modernism in art, he was seen as a painter whose works belonged in the attic along with the scrapbook of the Centennial Exhibition, brightly glazed majolica cuspidors, and great-aunt Lillian's tucked and embroidered wedding dress and hand-painted fan. It is revealing that although George Cochran Lambdin and his father James Read Lambdin (1807–1889) lived and worked in close association throughout their respective careers, George's choice of subject matter was from the beginning distinctly different from that of his father, whose reputation was built on state portraiture.[3] This is probably an indication of the degree of George's response to artistic and social currents, as well as an expression of his own very personal artistic direction.

The Early Works and the Genre Subjects

George was born in Pittsburgh on January 6, 1830, and was not yet ten years old when his family moved to Philadelphia in the late 1830s. In all probability James Lambdin gave his sons artistic instruction at a young age, and by 1852— or about the time of his twenty-second birthday—George was listed as "Portrait Painter," working at the same address as his father in Philadelphia. Four years earlier when he was only eighteen, he had exhibited three paintings at the Pennsylvania Academy of the Fine Arts: *Children Playing, Study of a Head,* and *Dorcas Distributing Garments to the Poor,* now unlocated and unavailable for study. Exhibition records for the next several years list numerous similar paintings—all of which are presently lost to us.

By 1850 the Lambdin family had settled in Germantown, a few miles northwest of central Philadelphia. Then, the family numbered eight: James R. Lambdin; his wife Mary Cochran (ca. 1810–1866); George Cochran; Eleanor Prudence (1832–1888); Annie, later Mrs. Augustus B. Snyder (1838–1910); James Harrison (1840–1870); Emma Connor (1843–1923); and Alfred Cochran (1846–1911). A seventh child, Agnes Marie, was born after 1850 and died after 1923. (An eighth child, Mary, was born in Pittsburgh ca. 1834 and lived only two years; and a ninth child, Alice, about whom nothing is known, was born in the early 1840s.)[4]

During the mid-1850s, when he was about twenty-five years old, George traveled in Europe, leaving home in late 1854 or very early 1855, perhaps somewhat earlier than historians have believed; by February 1855 he was studying in Munich with another young artist, William Henry Furness, Jr. (1827–1867). In May he "sent home several small pictures . . . which evince a strong feeling for color, and considerable poetic feeling." It is possible that both *Girls and Flowers* (1855; cat. 2) and *Girl in a Lavender Dress* (cat. 1) were among these. Although Lambdin's exact itinerary in Europe is unknown, he had apparently returned by late 1856; a December report described a new painting in his Philadelphia studio, "his best work": *Two Persons Talking by a Window in Twilight* (unlocated).[5] In composition, color, and use of light to define shape and form, Lambdin's paintings from the mid- and late-fifties suggest the influence of Dutch art, which he undoubtedly saw and carefully studied when in Europe.

One of George Cochran Lambdin's most notable early works was exhibited in Philadelphia while he was abroad in 1855, in New York two years later, and at the Royal Academy, London, in 1858. Its title, *Our Sweetest Songs Are Those That Tell of Saddest Thought* (fig. 1), is extracted from verse 18 of Percy Bysshe

Shelley's "To a Skylark":
> We look before and after
> And pine for what is not;
> Our sincerest laughter with some pain is fraught;
> Our sweetest songs are those that tell of saddest thought.[6]

This small painting shows a young woman playing a piano. She glances toward a standing girl, a vocalist, who, overcome with the pathos of the song, has buried her face in her hands. Her handkerchief is strategically placed on a chair beside her, and the message in underscored by the hourglass on the piano. A reviewer in *The Crayon* offers a contemporary critique:

Fig. 1 OUR SWEETEST SONGS ARE THOSE THAT TELL OF SADDEST THOUGHT, 1857
oil on canvas, 17¼ × 14 inches (43.9 × 35.5 cm.)
Courtesy of the Collection of the National Academy of Design, New York

3 CLASPING A BRACELET, 1857. *Courtesy of the Kennedy Galleries, New York*

The great charm [of this painting] consists in its being a simple incident, so truly [sic] and artistically embodied that sympathy for it is excited at once without any other suggestion or explanation. The figures are carefully studied, generally well drawn, and the entire picture conscientiously painted, and the color is good. . . . The subject is poetically treated. In the standing figure the concealing of emotion by placing the hands over the face is a fine point, also the introduction of the hour-glass on the piano. We should prefer to see a little more grace in the head of the performer at the piano. For sentiment this picture is Mr. Lambdin's best work; it is thoroughly original, and it excites the strongest faith in his future efforts.[7]

It is significant that this reviewer in 1857 singles out "sentiment" as a criterion for judging painting. This work is an early ancestor of Thomas Eakins's somewhat more restrained *The Pathetic Song* (1881). Both works convey to the viewer a sense of having entered a confined and enclosed space which is suffused with contained emotion.

Both figures in *Our Sweetest Songs* are dressed in high-style fashion for the 1850s; their clothing is cut from rather expensive goods, perhaps silk, and trimmed with lace. Similarly attired is the slim young woman in *Clasping a Bracelet* (1857; cat. 3), who seems to be the same woman who stands in *Our Sweetest Songs.*[8]

Within the next year or so, George Lambdin, not yet thirty years old, was asked to contribute an image for John W. Ehninger's *Autograph Etchings by American Artists*, published in 1859. The stated purpose of this volume was to introduce the *cliché verre* to the American public.[9] Lambdin was in good company. Fellow contributors included John Frederick Kensett, Asher Brown Durand, Eastman Johnson, Sanford Robinson Gifford, and Emanuel Leutze. Each artist illustrated a short poetic selection. Kensett illustrated a selection titled "Autumn," by J. R. Lowell; Durand, "The Pool," by F. S. Cozzens; Johnson, "The Wigwam," by Charles Sprague; Gifford, "Spring," by N. P. Willis, and Lambdin, "Childhood," by Thomas William Parsons:

> With us, the story's the reverse:
> Our souls are born already strung;
> But, 'twixt the cradle and the hearse,
> Creeps a change o'er us—for the worse!
> Our heart has music only when 'tis young.

Lambdin's image (cat. A) shows a small girl supporting a figure of an elephant for another child who sketches it. At one side a boy watches the sketch materialize. Lambdin's illustration is based on his oil painting entitled *Drawing the Elephant*, now in the National Academy of Design. The process had been suggested to Ehninger by an article from *Coelnischer Zeitung*, which had recommended the medium because it allows an artist to reproduce his own work without intervention of an engraver. No review of Lambdin's contribution to *Autograph Etchings* has been discovered; however, a critic who saw *Drawing the Elephant*, when exhibited the following year, found Lambdin's "child-subjects" remarkable for "naiveté of expression."[10]

After twice being nominated, once in 1855 and once in 1859, Lambdin was accepted as an associate of the Pennsylvania Academy of the Fine Arts. Four years later, in 1863, he was elected as an academician, a prestigious honor.[11]

By the early 1860s Lambdin had begun to exhibit—both at the Pennsylvania Academy and the National Academy of Design—the genre subjects and themes from childhood for which he became so well known.

In the second half of the nineteenth century, many aspects of American life were quite different from what they had been at the beginning of the century. With industrialization and urbanization came increasing affluence for many families; patterns of domestic life changed as fathers and heads of families were increasingly involved in business endeavors which freed their wives and children from the dawn-to-dark chores of rural life. Women had new leisure; children, more freedom. The move toward greater urbanization, particularly in the Eastern states, was accompanied by a powerful nostalgia for the "simplicity" and "nature" which were suddenly deemed inherent in agrarian community life of the past. Writers such as Ralph Waldo Emerson and Henry David Thoreau spoke of the values of the natural world and the simple life. In the 1860s and 1870s "wildness" was generally admired. Unspoiled nature which had previously been viewed as something to conquer or tame was reevaluated and labeled romantic and enticing. Throughout the century a taste for landscape painting (panoramic mountain vistas or intimate views of woodland foliage) and genre painting (simple narratives involving family life and children's activities) became increasingly popular.[12]

Children, no longer viewed as "little adults," were enjoyed for their endearing playfulness. Thoreau found in children's pastimes an honesty and joy so absent in the world of adult responsibilities and wrote, "Children, who play life, discern its true law and relations more clearly than men," and "Every child begins the world again." And Emerson remarked on "the engaging unconsciousness of childhood" which cannot be reflected upon "with regret or contempt."[13]

In the 1850s and 1860s, the decades of Little Eva, *Little Dorrit*, *Little Women*, and countless popular short stories in which children were the protagonists, Lambdin repeatedly depicted children's activities. One of his favorite themes seems to have been children painting or sketching, as in his *The Bashful Model* (cat. 5), which he completed in the fall of 1862. (It should be noted here that titles assigned to Lambdin's paintings are nearly always his own; they have

Cat. A   Childhood, 1859
Courtesy of the Rare Books Division,
Library of Congress

come down to us not only through the exhibition record but also from his fortunate habit of titling, signing, and dating most of his works on the stretcher or back of the canvas. {In addition, most of his works are signed and dated on the lower front, frequently in red}). A work completed seven years later is very similar in conception, although brighter in palette: *The Amateur Circus* (1869; cat. 16). Both paintings show a child's world—a world in which children participate without adult supervision or interference. We are unseen observers of secret, unselfconscious pursuits. As with his earlier paintings there is a sense of containment, as if the action were hermetically sealed off, untouched by the outside world.

Among other early surviving genre works focusing on children are *A Marvelous Story* (1861), *Sitting in the Sun, Germantown* (1862; cat. 6), *A Reading Party* (1862), *A Recruiting Party* (exhibited 1864), and *The New Knife* (exhibited Philadelphia Artists' Fund Society, 1866).[14] In *Sitting in the Sun, Germantown*, a pensive tyke (Lambdin's subjects, however young, so often are lost in thought) sits upon the rough stone stair in front of an open doorway which frames his head and shoulders. The foliage and flower which lean toward the child soften the image. Reading, or a subject with a book, was another frequently used theme. *A Marvelous Story* illustrates several children, accompanied by an exotic bird, absorbed in a storybook. *The Reading Party* shows two children attentively listening to an older child who reads aloud. *The New Knife* is an out-of-doors composition in which an older boy carves or whittles, admired by two younger onlookers. Beyond a fence lies a rural landscape of deeper pictorial space than in most of the artist's paintings.

On the theme of reading but showing an adult with children is the beautifully composed *Learning the Alphabet* (cat. 4) which shows two engrossed children learning letters from a book held by a comely and sedate young mother, aunt, or governess who is seated in profile. Her silhouette, echoed by the lower chair-back, forms an interesting compositional balance for the architectural details of the domestic interior. The light falls full upon the faces of the children as though to emphasize their enlightenment by learning. In the genre studies, Lambdin's women are poised and refined, with an ideal, madonna-like beauty. Only a very few painters in nineteenth century art have endowed women with such quiet dignity.

During the Civil War the Sanitary Commission organized major fairs (similar to the periodic international exhibitions, although much smaller and more hastily organized), from which funds were provided for Union wounded. Lambdin contributed paintings such as *Blossoms, Blowing Bubbles*, and *The Convalescent*. He also contributed *Stolen Lily* (1864; cat. 7), a small oil painting which was once a page in a bound book for which two dozen or more artists created an image. Such albums were auctioned or presented to organizers of the fairs. The most famous of these was presented to Charlotte Cushman in appreciation for her work at the Philadelphia fair held in early summer 1864.[15]

Lambdin's *Lazy Bones* (cat. 13) and *Small Pets* (cat. 12) are both works of 1867. An often repeated theme of the artist was that of rest and convalescence, and in *Lazy Bones* he has captured the languorous pose of the child who stretches and looks up expectantly as if to welcome special attention. A new appreciation of Lambdin as a colorist will emerge from this exhibition. The intense salmon pink (a favorite of the artist) of the coverlet divides the canvas in half diagonally, and provides a foil for both the generous, ruffled white pillows and the child's warm flesh. Lambdin's composition is uncomplicated but strong. We are brought directly into the child's space and attracted by the prominent oblique line of the bedcover which contrasts her curving arms and the rounded billowing pillows.

The young lady in *Small Pets* bears a resemblance to the girl in *Lazy Bones*. Dressed in dark pinafore covering red dress and stockings, she sits in an antique chair with feet upon a large, leather-bound book. Nestled on her lap, in the "V" formed by the joined hands, are two kittens, one black, one white. Red was a popular choice for children's clothes and was considered especially attractive to the young, whose eyes, it was thought, had not yet attained adult visual capacity. Here the vivid color of the dress is repeated in the carpet. The child is framed by the chair and the strong verticals and horizontals of furnishings and architectural details. Children with pets were a recurrent theme for Lambdin at

6 SITTING IN THE SUN, GERMANTOWN, 1862
Courtesy of Henry Melville Fuller

that time. The next year, his work included at least one other of a child holding two kittens, while "poor old pussy looks up with an anxious, matronly air, to see what is to become of them."[16]

4 LEARNING THE ALPHABET, n.d. *Courtesy of C.G. Sloan & Company, Inc.*

5 THE BASHFUL MODEL, 1862
Courtesy of Kenneth Lux Gallery, New York

16 THE AMATEUR CIRCUS, 1869
Courtesy of the North Carolina Museum of Art, Raleigh

12 SMALL PETS, 1867. *Courtesy of Mr. and Mrs. Walter Rubin*

13 LAZY BONES, 1867. *Courtesy of Mr. and Mrs. Richard Trotter*

The Civil War Paintings

During the decade of the sixties Lambdin's oeuvre was enriched by a series of paintings inspired by the war. These are paintings of especially fine quality which address a human and psychological aspect of the war rather than historical or military events. Although collectors and historians have frequently assumed that Lambdin played a significant role in the war, there is no evidence that this was the case. As a portrait reveals (cat. B), the soldier in these is Lambdin's younger brother, James Harrison ("Harry") Lambdin, who enlisted in the 121st Regiment, Army of the Potomac, in August 1862, and mustered out, then colonel, in September 1865. Harry Lambdin was himself an artist, and George was apparently much concerned about his brother's welfare. In the fall of 1863, Brig. Gen. James C. Rice wrote a letter (cat. C) assuring George of his brother's safety and advising George that Rice had applied for Harry's transfer to his staff as a "permanent fixture." However, the young captain was wounded in June 1864, so seriously that he received permission to return home temporarily for surgical treatment. Fifteen months later when the younger Lambdin left the service, he abandoned his artistic career, taught English at Episcopal Academy, near Philadelphia, and was ordained a Deacon in the Episcopal Diocese of Pennsylvania.[17]

At the Front (fig. 2) was exhibited at the National Academy of Design in 1866, where it was offered for sale by the artist. Here the officer, seated in front of a tent, stares broodingly into a campfire. The scene tells little of a soldier's activities—but speaks volumes about loneliness and separation from family. Separation was also the theme of a painting done the year before entitled, *The Consecration, 1861* (1865; cat. 10). A serious young woman kisses the sword of her departing uniformed sweetheart as he looks on. This is a complex painting richly filled with patterns of the oriental carpet and the room's accessories. The contrast between the woman's softly falling dress and the soldier's stark uniform is a focal point. Behind the couple stands a vase with floral bouquet, and in the left background is a rather clumsy reproduction of the *Venus de Milo*. The same statue (seen from a similar viewpoint) appears in Thomas C. Farrer's portrait of Clarence Cook (ca. 1861). Cook, an acquaintance of Lambdin's, was a New York critic associated with the Pre-Raphaelite movement in America. Thus, in addition to its obvious allusion to the relationship between officer and young woman, this Venus has tentative Pre-Raphaelite connections.

An oil sketch of the head and shoulders of a young woman entitled *Winter Quarters in Virginia—1864-5* (1866; cat. 11) is closely related to *The Consecration*. Possibly a study for this painting, one uncompleted, or one now lost, it provides a valuable opportunity to examine Lambdin's working methods and the sureness of brushstroke which later brought him success as a painter of flowers.

Weary, Tiresome Winter Quarters—Culpeper CO., VA. (1864; cat. 8) exemplifies the quality of war-related paintings. Surrounded by personal effects, a Union officer, lost in reverie, gazes into a fire. The log and canvas army quarters, with simple post-and-lintel fireplace, make-shift shelving, and rectangular entrance to a partially visible bunkroom, form a compositional framework around the pensive officer. Iconographical details intensify the mood of melancholy, regret for lost comrades, and longing for loved ones: a snuffed candle upon the mantel, three prominent swords, framed portraits suggesting absent family, and a sheet of paper, perhaps a letter from home which slipped from his fingers as he became lost in thought. The mellow browns of the room interior, a few golden highlights, and a repetition of the red of the glowing fire in the coverings of the bunks lend a sense of warmth and heightened emotion.[18] Another, almost identical, version of this work is dated 1866: *Winter Quarters in Virginia—Army of the Potomac, 1864.*

The *Winter Quarters* pictures may have stemmed from an actual visit George paid to his brother (it was common for family members to pay such visits). There is documentation that George traveled south at least twice, in early 1864 and again in summer 1865; from these trips he is reported to have brought home "interesting studies of camp life" which would serve as "material for future work."[19]

Fig. 2 AT THE FRONT, 1866
oil on canvas, 18¹/₄ × 24 inches (46.36 × 60.96 cm.)
Courtesy of the Detroit Institute of Arts, Founders Society Purchase, Director's Discretionary Fund

CAPTAIN JAMES HARRISON LAMBDIN

Cat. B   Portrait of Captain James Harrison Lambdin.
Courtesy of Richard C. Carter, Wilmington, Delaware

10 THE CONSECRATION 1861, 1865
Courtesy of the Indianapolis Museum of Art: James E. Roberts Fund

Critical Reception at the Paris Universal Exhibition:
The Last Sleep

In 1867, *Consecration, 1861* (cat. 10), then the property of George Whitney, was sent to the Paris Universal Exposition along with *The Last Sleep,* probably the same as a painting of 1858 which has also been titled *The Dead Wife* (fig. 3). This large painting shows a lovely young woman (perhaps the same as the subject of *Our Sweetest Songs* (fig. 1) and *Clasping a Bracelet* (cat. 3) just deceased. She lies in an enclosed space in which the most prominent details are a multipaned window, one side slightly ajar, a bouquet of flowers, and a small statue of an angel. By her bed is her grieving husband or lover who, as noted by the French critic Paul Mantz, is "almost dead himself." Mantz's review dwells at length on the "poignant emotion" and the details of the events which he imagines led up to the young woman's death.[20]

The first time Lambdin exhibited his image of the deceased woman (1858) at the Pennsylvania Academy, he titled it with five lines taken from the final stanza of Tennyson's "The Deserted House,"

> . . . Life and thought
> Here no longer dwell
> But in a city glorious
> A great and distant city they have bought
> A mansion incorruptible.

A critic who reviewed it then, found the painting worthy of "unqualified admiration," for its "spiritual impression," and decided its "power of imagination" was "unsurpassed by any work of the day." He said:

> The objects emblematic of or associated with the subject—the flowers by the bedside, and the statuette of an angel placed upon a bracket over head of the bed, scarcely visible in the darkened chamber, are appropriately introduced; while the gloom of the apartment into which the spectator looks, and the half-light of the outer room beyond, which is faintly illuminated through closed blinds, showing a bright gleam of sunlight reflected upon the window-sash, its rays finding their way across the pillow whereon the head of the wife rests,—all this is rendered with wonderful truth and feeling.[21]

Fig. 3 THE DEAD WIFE (THE LAST SLEEP), n.d.
oil on canvas, 40 × 54 inches (101.6 × 137.2 cm.)
Courtesy of the North Carolina Museum of Art, Gift of Peter A. Vogt

Another American critic, Henry Tuckerman, responded to its pathos in the year it was sent to Paris: "The blinds are drawn; the fair youthful form lies stilled in death, and the husband, utterly crushed with grief, has flung himself across the bed. His face is not seen, but we can image its pallor, even as in fancy we can hear the choking sobs with which his bosom heaves."[22]

Deaths or anticipated deaths were a favorite theme in American art, literature, and music in the Victorian era and especially in the 1860s; and of course the new medium of photography was frequently employed to capture a final image of a deceased or terminally ill loved one. In spite of the losses of the Civil War, very young children, youthful wives, and mothers of all ages were those with whom our artists, poets, and songwriters were most concerned. (Writing about music, Sigmund Spaeth has commented, "One finds a plethora of mid-Victorian grief for both sexes, although the assumption generally is that gentlemen do not die.")[23]

In shape and composition, Lambdin's *Last Sleep* closely resembles *The Death of Chatterton* (1856) by the English Pre-Raphaelite painter Henry Wallis. Indeed, the arch-top canvas was used in numerous Pre-Raphaelite works, especially those whose content or emotional message required that they be so dignified, such as Sir John Everett Millais's, *Ophelia* (1852) and William Holman Hunt's *The Light of the World*. And of course, the curved shape of the stereoscopic view and the shape into which early photographic portraits were framed or cut may have influenced Lambdin's choice of shape.

Wallis's *Death of Chatterton* had just been published as a wood engraving in a popular English magazine. Two other British images may have also influenced Lambdin's choice of subject matter and composition in his *Last Sleep*. Sir Joseph Noël Paton's *The Dead Lady* (early 1850s) shows a dark-haired female figure stretched horizontally across the picture space. At her head are draperies, as in Lambdin's painting, and at her side (although on the viewer's side of the picture space) is a mourning figure leaning over the body. In 1858 Henry Peach Robinson, an English photographer, created a work he titled *Fading Away*. A composite of five negatives, the work shows a dying young woman, not unlike Lambdin's dead woman, surrounded by despairing family in a horizontal composition with a window in the background. Robinson accompanied his image with a stanza from Shelley.[24]

The Late Sixties

The late 1860s were a transitional period for Lambdin. His mother's death in 1866 may have discouraged him from traveling to Paris for the 1867 exhibition; however, soon he left his family's home in Germantown for New York City where he took up residence in the Tenth Street Studio Building, then an important center of artistic activity. The artists' quarters at 51 West Tenth Street provided suitable studio space, a fraternal atmosphere and the benefits of group exhibitions. Lambdin was at the studio in late 1867 (whether as a visitor or regular occupant is unknown), and during the following spring occupied John Ferguson Weir's quarters. He also may have shared a studio with John La Farge, a significant alliance because Lambdin turned to flower painting shortly thereafter. Once Weir returned, Lambdin probably extended his stay by taking over Jervis McEntee's room during summer and perhaps longer. He had been "anxious to obtain a footing" at 51 West Tenth Street, and at least some degree of success must have been his; during 1868 he was elected an academician at the National Academy of Design. Other artists then in residence at the studio included John George Brown and Seymour Joseph Guy.[25]

Probably under their influence, and of others such as Eastman Johnson and Winslow Homer, who were also in New York, he continued to specialize in the genre subjects which had constituted the greater part of the early oeuvre. It is impossible, of course, to determine if certain works dated 1868 or 1869 and exhibited then may have had an earlier, Philadelphia origin. But aside from a portrait of his colleague Enoch Wood Perry (1869; fig. 4), exhibition records and reviews indicate that his specialization continued to be genre painting.

The Pruner (1868; fig. 5) and *Playmates* (1868; cat. 14) fall into this group of unknown origin. They appear to be Germantown subjects and Lambdin had exhibited paintings entitled *The Pruner* at the Pennsylvania Academy in 1864 and in February 1867 at the Artists' Fund Society of Philadelphia. Perhaps there were several versions of *The Pruner*—as is true for certain other genre subjects. Or perhaps Lambdin sometimes worked over a painting, exhibiting it in what was not to be its final state before dating it. This may also have been the case with *Our Sweetest Songs*, exhibited first in 1855 but dated 1857. *Playmates* illustrates a preadolescent girl, clad in soft lavender-grey and holding

Fig. 4 ENOCH WOOD PERRY, 1869
oil on canvas mounted on masonite, 30 × 25 inches (76.2 × 63.5 cm)
Courtesy of the Collection of the National Academy of Design, New York

Fig. 5 THE PRUNER, 1868
oil on canvas, 24 × 20 inches (61 × 50.8 cm)
Courtesy of the Museum of Fine Arts, Boston

a spray of autumn leaves, which she seems to contemplate. Intent on her reverie is a very white, almost artificial dog, her "playmate." Although posed against a neutral wall, the girl is skillfully framed by the void of an entryway and a vine which climbs at her side and cascades downward over her head.

In the well-known *The Pruner* an older man clips a high branch while a boy of about four or five years old looks on intently. As in his other genre scenes the viewer feels the arrested motion, the sense of the artist's having captured an

7 A STOLEN LILY, 1864
Courtesy of M.R. Schweitzer, Schweitzer Gallery, New York

14 PLAYMATES, 1868
Courtesy of R.H. Love Galleries, Inc.

24

15 THE VINEYARD, n.d.
Courtesy of The J.M. Smucker Company, Orrville, Ohio

intimate moment of which we are allowed a glimpse. Although the activity, that of cutting back a tree, is a common one, the scene is not simply a genre scene but an exploration of the relationship between generations. The child is fascinated with the work and skills of the adult, and to some extent, the place of work and chores in the adult world. With the child we turn to look at the man, and his work attains a new dignity. As with many of Lambdin's other pictures, we view the scene as uninvited visitors, and we participate from a child's point of view.

Another work that cannot yet be securely dated, but which may have been painted as early as 1868, is *The Vineyard* (cat. 15), a typical outdoor setting, with a figure framed by verdant foliage within which red-skinned grapes provide effective color contrast. The model is almost certainly the same one who posed for *Playmates*. And the exhibition records show that in 1868–1869 Lambdin displayed a "Figure, Eating Grapes," dated 1868, at an exhibition of the Cincinnati Academy of Fine Arts.

In the summer or fall of 1868, Lambdin had done some painting out-of-doors, for at the winter exhibition of the National Academy he brought "from his country rambles" sketches and "partly-finished pictures." These included *Wild Fruit,* described as "a very cunning sketch of a little girl leaning against a fence and eating a bunch of wild grapes."[26] In this instance we are again confused by Lambdin's tendency to repeat themes and subjects, making only slight changes but assigning a new title. (And, of course, both reviewers and collectors have sometimes furnished titles of their own preference, thus further complicating the issue.) In 1869 Louis Prang & Company issued a chromolithograph entitled *Wild Fruit* (cat. 18) after an unspecified Lambdin painting. In the chromolithograph, a small girl stands barefoot before a tree; she holds and eats grapes from a wild vine which climbs over the tree's high branches. She does not, however, lean on a fence which is described by the reviewer who saw the Lambdin painting called *Wild Fruit* in early 1869. The Prang lithograph, however, is quite similar to a small oil painting called *In the Garden* (dated 1869), one of six Lambdin paintings in the collection of the National Academy of Design.

Prang issued *Wild Fruit* as a companion piece to Eastman Johnson's *Barefoot Boy,* a very popular and widely distributed chromolithograph based on John Greenleaf Whittier's poem of the same name. Lambdin's work very likely illustrates lines 33–35 from the same poem:

> Where the freshest berries grow,
> Where the ground-nut trails its vine,
> Where the wood-grape's clusters shine.

Thoreau had once written: "Berries are just beginning to ripen, and children are planning expeditions after them. They are important as introducing children to the fields and woods, and as wild fruits of which much account is made. During the berry season the schools have a vacation, and many little fingers are busy picking these small fruits. It is ever a pastime, not a drudgery."

Another theme of children in nature is fishing. In 1869 Lambdin exhibited *The Experienced Fisherman*, which was described at that time as "a small upright piece of still life, if such a term may be applied to human beings. . . . Three boys make up the group. One is baiting his hook, watched the while, with absorbing interest, by a petticoated tyro at his side. The third, statue-like and soberly tinted, is intent upon his business. All is harmonious, quiet, natural, truthful, yet withall original. . . ."[27]

Fishing is hardly an original theme in American art, for there were numerous precedents. But the perfect balanced stillness of the children is peculiar to Lambdin's work, which may explain the critic's description "original." Whether or not *The Experienced Fisherman* is quite similar or identical to the *Biddle Children Fishing on the Schuylkill*, of the same year, is unknown; however, Lambdin's *A Good Day for Sunnies* (1868; cat. E) relates directly to the *Biddle Children*, except in the details of the bridge, and an unfinished quality in the face of one child.[28]

In the 1870s Lambdin continued to produce delightful genre paintings and child studies, although many were derived from ideas of earlier years. *A Child of the Sun* (1874; cat. 31) is a descendent of his *A Stolen Lily* and *Wild Fruit*. And, *Little White Heifer* (1876; cat. 34) returns to the same theme of *White Heifer Calf* (1869; cat. 17) although the later work shows improvement in color and composition.

But in a general sense, however, his residency in New York marked the end of his emphasis on genre, for soon thereafter his work took important new directions.

Exactly when Lambdin's stay at Tenth Street Studios ended is unknown; however, in spring or early summer of 1870 he and his brother Harry left for Europe. Travel on the Continent was complicated by the Franco-Prussian War, so they moved to England, but Harry's health began to fail rapidly. Two months after their enforced return home, James Harrison Lambdin died in November 1870 at the age of thirty.[29]

17 WHITE HEIFER CALF, 1869
Courtesy of the Artemis Gallery

New Directions: Flowers and Studies of Women

The artist did not exhibit at the National Academy in 1870, 1871, or 1872 (and, of course, the Pennsylvania Academy had cancelled its annuals in those years as it prepared to move to new quarters). Lambdin did show some paintings in the years 1870 to 1872, but, understandably, not so many as in the past. Between 1871 and 1875, he created some of the floral masterpieces for which he is best known today, indicating that within a short time he had not only taken an entirely new direction, but also that he met with immediate success. The reasons for Lambdin's seemingly abrupt change in subject emphasis in about 1870 or 1871 are open to question. When in New York City, he would have known painters working in a variety of genres, among them some experimenting with floral works. And we know that he had at least an acquaintance and perhaps even a close temporary association with John La Farge at 51 West Tenth Street.[30]

The power in La Farge's flower images might well have aroused Lambdin's lingering desire to specialize in flower painting, and to enlarge on the floral themes which had constituted part of his earlier oeuvre, often in combination with figure studies as in his *Girls and Flowers* (cat. 2). And although the circumstances of the 1870 trip as we now know them would suggest that the turmoil of the war and the distress of Harrison's illness precluded the absorption of much culture, it is also true that his trip to Europe may have acquainted him with the work of French flower painters.

But there is another reason why he may have become encouraged to become a flower painter (in addition to the growing popular demand for such paintings, which made still lifes more marketable). Philadelphia at that time was considered a city of flowers; and Germantown was the garden center of the city. The general Philadelphia area was a "hotbed" of horticultural activity in which both professionals and amateurs participated. Founded in 1827, the Pennsylvania Horticultural Society fostered competitions and exhibitions and provided information and instruction. By the end of the century many of those most active in the Society's affairs maintained gardens in Germantown. Thomas Meehan (1826–1901), lectured widely, was editor of the *Gardener's Monthly* for thirty years, wrote the monumental *Native Flowers and Ferns of the United States* which was published by Louis Prang & Company in 1878–1879, and maintained

extensive nurseries in Germantown, with which Lambdin certainly would have been familiar. And if Germantown was a floral center, above all it was a center of rose culture, especially at the height of the hybrid tea rose craze in the early 1870s. In 1874, Germantown's C. P. Hayes, one of the founders of the nursery company of Miller & Hayes, wrote a short series of articles for *The Horticulturist* recommending various varieties of new roses, hybrids from here and abroad. This Germantown nursery was called the largest cultivator of new roses in this country, and became so famous internationally that the noted European rose grower, E. Verdier, in 1873, named a select seedling "The Miller & Hayes Rose." By the early 1870s, George Cochran Lambdin would have been quite literally surrounded by roses and rose-talk. Moreover, George Lambdin and his family, with considerable professional assistance from the English gardener William Cochrane, cultivated flowers, especially "select" roses, in the gardens of their Price Street home.[31]

Although some of Lambdin's most successful and spectacular floral paintings are of flowers other than the rose, the great majority of his flower studies are of roses, and indeed he was known in his own day for "Lambdin's roses," in both oil and watercolor. Apparently he was deeply attached to the rose, for he wrote an essay entitled, "The Charm of the Rose."[32]

Lambdin's floral studies fall into several basic categories. First, there are the traditional table-top still lifes, such as the two versions of *Roses in an Oriental Vase* (cat. 35 and 36), *Still Life* (cat. 38) or his *Apple Blossoms* (cat. 22). In Lambdin's oeuvre, this type of still life is generally set in a shallow picture space, with no emphasis at all on the surroundings. Vases are either of Oriental ceramic, a popular type of Chinese export celadon, or simple glass containers. Often, Lambdin used the same vase over and over, and to accommodate very different types of flowers, an indication that displaying the flowers was more important than vessels and surroundings. In one late work which is known only from a photograph (cat. M), Lambdin has painted two containers—a hobnail glass and a slim cordial glass, set side by side at a window, each filled with roses, and even the photograph suggests a lush texture of dark petals against light.

21 ROSES, 1872
Courtesy of Yale University Art Gallery,
Gift of Jo Ann and Julian Ganz, Jr.

37 ROSES, 1876
Courtesy of The Arden Collection

41 ROSES AND WHITE AZALEAS, 1877
Courtesy of Frank S. Schwarz & Son, Philadelphia

A second kind of still life in which the artist specialized is the "Ruskinian" study—flowers shown growing, as in nature, against a sky or a wall. *Roses on a Wall* (1874; cat. 23) is a fine example and may be the painting of the same title that Lambdin sent to the Paris exhibition in 1878. A second spectacular example is *June Roses* (1879; cat. 47). And yet another is the lovely watercolor study on brown paper (1880s; cat. 50), one of the few works in this medium by the artist which can be identified today.

Like John La Farge, Lambdin also painted water lilies. A Ruskinian study looking down on American pond lilies, entitled *A Wind on the Lily Pond* (fig. 6), is reminiscent of titles La Farge used.[33] Lambdin may have done a second such painting, exhibited at the National Academy in 1874 as *Lily Pond, New Jersey*. Water lilies had captured the popular attention earlier in the century and there was continuing interest in exotic varieties, but Lambdin depicted simpler American versions growing in nature. An interesting sidelight to this theme is the fact that in 1870 the Philadelphia School of Design for Women offered its students "4 casts [of the] water lily" to draw from.[34]

A variation on the Ruskinian study is the greenhouse arrangement, in which a group of potted flowering plants are shown as in a hothouse or conservatory, as for example in his *Autumn Sunshine* (1880; cat. 48) a splendid array of yellow and pink chrysanthemums planted in terra-cotta pots. Stems and tendrils of a vine, growing from an unseen location, enter the composition from the right and with pleasing angularity move across the canvas to the upper left. In this, as in at least one other Ruskinian still life, the 1877 *Roses on a Wall* now in the Ganz collection, Lambdin has, perhaps unwisely, included a butterfly. Exhibition records note that he showed *A Group of Plants* in Brooklyn in 1878 and *Side of a Greenhouse* in Louisville in 1878 and Philadelphia in 1879. His painting *In The Greenhouse* (cat. 49) must date from the late seventies or perhaps even the eighties. On the floor of the greenhouse sit four clay pots. The largest, at right rear, supports the stalks of a calla lily plant, of which two full flowers form a canopy over a third, not-yet open bloom. Balancing this on the left is a spindly rose stem supporting a closed bud which forms a "V" with an unflowered branch. This rose bush has two flowers, the larger of which pulls the eye to the center of the canvas. The center of the painting, and its focal point, is the full-flowered azalea plant, its broadly painted pink flowers in full bloom. To the right, dipping to the lower corner of the canvas, is a more sparsely flowered red azalea. Two of its blossoms (barely suggested) have fallen to the floor. Thus the hanging, soon-to-disintegrate yellow rose balances the lilies—its downward pull creates an opposition to the callas' upward thrust. Perhaps the most notable feature of the painting is the combination of the substantial stems of the lily

35 ROSES IN AN ORIENTAL VASE, 1876
Courtesy of Richard C. Carter, Wilmington, Delaware

48 AUTUMN SUNSHINE, 1880
*Courtesy of the National Museum of American Art,
Smithsonian Institution*

with the softer, weaker, delicately defined azaleas and roses, which, as a group, diagonally cross the canvas.

Still another type of floral still life is that with black or solid dark background, of which the present exhibition includes many examples—both oil paintings and chromolithographs. These are, in a general sense, related to botanical illustration, especially the full-colored frontispieces which were common by the seventies. The blossoms, usually of a single plant, grow in an upright position and often show various stages of development (buds through full bloom). Botanical illustration, however, is generally done against a white or plain background. But Lambdin had experimented with various supports, among them slate and tin which may have suggested a solid dark background. Prang and Lambdin must have agreed that a solid colored background (blue, green, or black) intensified the delicacy, textures, and color of floral studies. In the years following the 1869 reproduction of *Wild Fruit* Prang marketed many such Lambdin floral studies, five of which are included in this exhibition (cat. 46, 29, 30, 44, 25).[35]

The process by which the chromolithographs were produced is illustrated in a series of progressive proofs (cat. 26). An overview of the process, and the knowledge that more than thirty states were required to produce a floral image, in this case *White Lily* (cat. 25) would suggest that the process was so complicated that the lithographers' efforts were centered on the flowers themselves, which showed to best advantage against a solid background and especially a black one.

The effectiveness of this aesthetic is well demonstrated by *Calla Lilies* (1874; cat. 27), a masterpiece in which the solid black background enhances the grandeur. Every nuance of the stark green leaves shows to advantage. And the gradually unfurling shapes are textured, living, and touchable. They almost move into the viewer's space. This rare example is a great masterpiece for in its insistent directness and simplicity it embodies a modernity never hinted at in his other works. Another example of calla lilies from the same year (cat. 28) was painted on a tin support. Prang & Company, also in 1874, issued a chromolithograph after Lambdin's callas (cat. 29). Lambdin had been drawn to this flower earlier in his career: in 1864 he exhibited *Callas* at the Pennsylvania Academy.

Roses and White Azaleas (1877, cat. 41), another work on black enameled panel, emphasizes the lush and fragile beauty of petals and stamens. These black-background floral studies are among the most successful of all nineteenth-century flower paintings.

Studies of women were a second area that claimed his attention in the 1870s and 1880s. The examples selected for this exhibition combine girls and flowers but in other respects they are quite different from one another.

In 1872 Lambdin painted *A Young Girl Reading* (cat. 19). Two years later he offered it for sale at the National Academy. Horace Fairbanks purchased it for the St. Johnsbury Athenaeum, where it has hung for more than one hundred years. It is difficult to view the painting without thinking of the progress of photography at that time, for in static pose, arrangement of furniture and accessories, and interior space it is very reminiscent of the cabinet portrait so popular in the early seventies. One is also reminded of the reclusive, physically isolated existence of Emily Dickinson (1830–1886), whose mature years would have been contemporaneous with Lambdin's late paintings of women. Moreover, almost all of Lambdin's themes have parallels in the popular literature of the time. To give a single example, in early 1876 an American magazine of widespread circulation published a feature article entitled "Woman a Mystery," in which the author points to the impotence of women as adults in society:

> Morally dissected, in search of a soul, [woman] has been physically dissected, that her maternal frame might be held to view as weak, as unenduring, as incapable of accomplishing her desires of progress. Yet [others] have one and all failed to learn the secrets of her being. Those are known to herself alone, and she does not hasten to reveal them. Her powers are not lessened that she does not proclaim what she is; the world is her own, and when the hour comes she will take possession of her own. . . . Into the outer court of the temple [men] may come, and may at times have approached the inner court, but into the holy of holies but one enters—herself. She alone is priestess and evangel of all its mysteries.[36]

Remote, self-contained, mysterious and enigmatic in her isolation, Lambdin's young woman seems sealed away from the world but nevertheless complete unto herself. That she is anonymous makes her to a certain extent symbolic and universal, thus heightening the sense of mystery.

Among the Roses (1877; cat. 42) is a beautiful outdoor composition in which a standing young girl, pinning a bloom to her hair, is framed by pink roses. An entirely different type of female image may be seen in *New Moon, True Moon, Trust I Say Who my True Love Must Be* (cat. 53). This is a late work in which two mature women look to the sky as though to settle a question of love or romance by reciting a rhythmic ditty to the rising moon. Lambdin must have done at least one other version of this theme in the mid-eighties, for in early 1886 a Philadelphia critic described his painting *Hesperus:* "Two young girls, blonde and brunette, are gazing up into the sunset sky, entranced by the radiant splendor of the evening star. The roseate flush of parting day suffuses their

19 A YOUNG GIRL READING, 1872
Courtesy of St. Johnsbury Athenaeum, St. Johnsbury, Vermont

uplifted faces and bare arms, and enhances the charm of their contrasted beauty." According to the reviewer, that painting was a "large upright figure piece," illustrating the subject "Hesperus, the star of Love,/The star of Love and Dreams." Thus, because of the upright format, it cannot be *New Moon.*[37]

Ruskinian Thought and Pre-Raphaelitism

Paintings such as *Roses on a Wall* (cat. 23), *June Roses* (cat. 47), and *A Wind on the Lily Pond* (fig. 6) encourage us to ask, "To what extent did Lambdin paint in response to the Pre-Raphaelite movement?" In 1857 a disappointed John Ruskin had written,

> I believe the most beautiful position in which flowers can possibly be seen is precisely their most natural one—low flowers relieved by grass or moss, and tree blossoms relieved against the sky. How it happens that no flower-painter has yet been moved to draw a cluster of boughs of peach blossom, or cherry blossom, or apple blossom just as they grow, with the deep blue sky between every bud and petal, is more than I can understand; except that I know, in art, the likeliest and properest thing for everybody to do is almost always the last that will be done.[38]

Although he had exhibited such works as *Wisteria on a Wall* as early as 1867 (Artists' Fund Society of Philadelphia), most of George Lambdin's Ruskinian still lifes did not materialize until much later, in the 1870s. They are mainly studies of roses, of which numerous examples are known. Some of his most successful works fall into this group and rank among the most sophisticated outdoor still lifes in American art. Lambdin depicts his growing flowers without undue artifice, but with that sure sense of composition which makes him a master. He does not set his flowers within a landscape, as Ruskin proposed, but rather brings them to the picture plane. We may learn something about these flowers as they grow in nature, for the artist carefully represents each stage of the blooming from newly formed buds to near-disintegration of the flower head, in keeping with Darwinian ideas. Strict realism is sacrificed to art, however, for the stalks and stems seem unnaturally tenuous: their graceful curving through the compositions adds a sense of delicacy.

Lambdin was not integrally connected with the Pre-Raphaelite leadership in America. But, through his acquaintance with William Trost Richards (1833–1905), he must have been aware of the movement from its inception. Richards, a Germantown resident and close family friend of the Lambdins, had espoused

Fig. 6 A WIND ON THE LILY POND, 1874
oil on canvas, 16 × 20 inches (40.6 × 50.8 cm)
Courtesy, © 1986 Sotheby's, Inc.

the quest for literal rendering of plant life painted or drawn out of doors before becoming a member of the Association for the Advancement of Truth in Art (the American counterpart of the Pre-Raphaelite Brotherhood in England) in 1863.[39] And the traveling exhibition of English art—which was so important in introducing English Pre-Raphaelitism to American artists—opened at the Pennsylvania Academy in February 1858, while James Lambdin chaired the Committee on Exhibitions. Later, George Lambdin exhibited works called *Beech Drops and Toad Stools* (1861) and *Dandelion Curls* (1865), which suggest the Pre-Raphaelite predilection for focusing on nature in its humblest aspects. In 1861, Harry Lambdin exhibited *A Narcissus: Study From Nature,* which may have had Pre-Raphaelite associations. George Lambdin's interest in children as "little adults" has counterparts in Pre-Raphaelite work, as for example in John Everett Millais's *My Second Sermon* (1864). There is also the similarity of format between Lambdin's *Last Sleep* and Wallis's *Death of Chatterton,* and a generic relationship between Lambdin's *Consecration, 1861* (cat. 10) and Millais's *The Huguenot* (1851–52). Moreover, like the Pre-Raphaelites, Lambdin used literary titles.

49 IN THE GREENHOUSE, n.d. *Courtesy of The Metropolitan Museum of Art, Gift of Mrs. J. Augustus Barnard*

Lambdin's correspondents included Clarence Cook, an active member of the American Pre-Raphaelite movement from the beginning. And Lambdin's early work was frequently reviewed—and kindly so—in *The Crayon*, the same magazine that routinely published letters and comments by John Ruskin and William Michael Rossetti, the philosopher brother of the painter Dante Gabriel Rossetti.

The New Path, the Pre-Raphaelite voice in America after *The Crayon's* demise in 1861, was known for its scathing reviews of those whose work it disapproved. One reviewer, possibly Clarence Cook, focused on Lambdin's *May Flowers* of 1863:

> It cannot be too late yet, Mr. Lambdin, but it will be soon! This picture of 'May Flowers' is the worst thing you have done yet, but, if you will now do as you promised five years ago, and paint a good picture, it will show to double advantage by the memory of this. Is it possible that you, too, have sheathed your sword, and given in to the prevailing notion that there comes a time when study may cease, and art begin? You are working as if you believed it, but we are very sure you do not. These pictures make us sorry more than angry. Only one thing we will say, that your work, such as it is, is not copied, but is your own, and, even now, if, instead of dreaming and theorizing, you would draw diligently, and let color go for a year or two, there is hope. But drawing is essential, and you do not know how to draw anything; hand nor foot, nor arm, nor face, no, not the least fold of a gown. A picture of the size and apparent importance of [this] ought not to have been attempted until after, at least, ten years of thoughtful, varied and unintermitting labor. And, even after such a service, only one picture of this size should have been painted in a year. It would take a year's hard thinking, and the result of a number of years' experience to fill so large a canvass with ideas enough, or sufficiently beautiful color or truthful drawing to make it worth its price. You smile, young artist! Well, so do your gray beard friends, A. and B. and C., who sell their works with less trouble than it took to paint them, for whatever sums they choose to charge; who never work, and never did work; who think only how many pictures they can paint and get rid of in a year, and would think you a hare-brained fanatic if you put a bit more conscientious labor into your picture than will suffice to make it sell.[40]

If George Cochran Lambdin henceforth paid close attention to Pre-Raphaelite precepts, it may have been in self-defense. But, however harsh, the reviewer's viewpoint was not unjustified. *May Flowers*, a depiction of a woman and child in a garden (now in the collection of the National Academy of Design) lacks the compositional and formal strength of earlier figure studies. And Lambdin was probably little inclined to strive painstakingly for the precision of detail which characterizes much Pre-Raphaelite work and which challenged his colleague Richards to labor over studies interminably. Nor is the degree of feeling in Lambdin's works like the heightened emotional tension of much Pre-Raphaelitism. Comparison of Lambdin's *Our Sweetest Songs, Consecration, 1861*, and *The Last Sleep* with such English works as Millais's The *Huguenot*, William Holman Hunt's *The Awakening Conscience* (1853) or Arthur Hughes's *April Love* (1855) makes this clear. Lambdin's works convey a feeling of sweet, poignant sentimentality or sorrow rather than conflict and strained painful tension.

George Cochran Lambdin and Photography

Another life-long interest of Lambdin was photography, and as early as 1862 he relied on photographs for many poses. Numerous figures in his work of that decade can be clearly related to extant albumin prints, many of which were taken as series of studies, to be used as the artist wished or the composition required. The photograph illustrated in figure 10, for example, is the study for the three-or-four year old girl in *The Bashful Model* (1862; cat. 5); the same child with slight changes of hairstyle and position (but not age) may be the model for the central figure in *The Amateur Circus* (1869; cat. 16). The young woman in Lambdin's *Rosy Reverie* (1865; cat. 9), and the woman in *The Consecration, 1861* (1865; cat. 10), and *Winter Quarters* (1866; cat. 11), the adult male in *The Pruner* (1868; fig. 5), and perhaps even the young woman in profile in *The Vineyard* (cat. 15) can all be related to the figural studies in the recently re-discovered photographs illustrated in figures 11–14 (cat. D). Even the spotless white calf in *Little White Heifer* (1876; cat. 34) has been copied from an albumin print of a very unprepossessing barnyard creature (fig. 15).[41]

In addition to the direct correspondence between Lambdin's figure subjects and specific photographs, there is a suggestion that Lambdin owned many more photographs. For example, the same small child, in white Garibaldi blouse falling freely over a salmon-colored skirt (which in turn covers another garment) is easily picked out, because of her distinctive white hooded headress in *The New Knife, The Amateur Circus* (1869; cat. 16), and *Little White Heifer* (1876; cat. 34).

8 WEARY, TIRESOME WINTER QUARTERS—CULPEPER CO., VA, 1864. *Courtesy of Richard C. Carter, Wilmington, Delaware*

2 GIRLS AND FLOWERS, 1855
Courtesy of the National Museum of American Art, Smithsonian Institution

34 LITTLE WHITE HEIFER, 1876
Courtesy of Lagakos Turak Gallery, Philadelphia

Although these paintings were painted over a span of about ten years, the child does not age, and continues to wear a garment that was high style in the 1860s (see figs. 8–9). This alone implies that Lambdin had a series of photographs of this child model in various poses dating from the 1860s.

Provocative evidence of artists' general attitudes towards using photographs as studies or models, and the suggestion of a trade in photographs between New York and Philadelphia is provided by a June 1862 letter from William Holbrook Beard (1824–1900) to "Mr. Lambden." Beard requested two photographs of cats (for which he enclosed the sum of $2.00). Beard first excused the request, saying "I do not use them in painting"; then contradicted himself: "But if I had a photograph which was what I wanted or could get one that would help me in my picture, I should not hesitate to use it. Nor would I care to conceal it." More revealingly, Beard added: "So I do not wish the Photographer to destroy the negative on my account." Lambdin had previously sent two animal photographs, probably also of cats, to Beard, who was now requesting two more from "the six remaining prints." Of the first two, "The expression of the one lying down I think is wonderfully fine, and altogether it formed a perfect little picture." At this juncture it is useful to note that Lambdin was also painting images of cats and kittens in the 1860s, for example, *Young Girl with a Cat* (1862) and his *Small Pets* (1867; cat. 12). Although George Lambdin's father James was also working from photographs by 1870, it is more likely that Beard's letter was addressed to the younger of the two.[42]

The maker of these amateur photographs is not known, but may have been one of the Lambdins or a member of their Philadelphia artistic circle. George's younger brother, Alfred, was a member of the Photographic Society of Philadelphia for a time between 1862 and 1883; and the Lambdins had close connections with at least a few of the many Philadelphia photographers active in this period, some of whom, like Frederick DeBourg Richards (1822–1903) and Peter Moran (1841–1914) were also painters. It is possible that Beard's request for photographs was not an isolated instance and that there was a more general trading of photographic studies between Philadelphia and New York artists during the 1860s and 1870s. There is a remarkable general similarity of the female figure in Winslow Homer's painting *The Initials* (1864) and the sturdy young woman who strikes several poses against a post in the group of photos owned by Lambdin (figs. 16–18). Homer's figure has braid trim (popular during the Civil War), which is not visible in the Lambdin photographs, but in all other respects (construction of clothing, coiffeur and hat, general proportions and posture, fall of draperies) the images are curiously similar. There is also a striking similarity

Fig. 7 Adolphe Braun (1811–1877) Flowers, circa 1856, albumin print from glass negative, 19¼ × 16⅜ inches (48.8 × 41.0 cm). *Courtesy of the International Museum of Photography at George Eastman House*

47 JUNE ROSES, 1879. *Courtesy of John H. Garzoli Fine Art, San Francisco*

between this series of photographs and the series of photographs made of Jane Morris for Dante Gabriel Rossetti in 1865.[43]

An example of a possible trading of photographs dating from the 1870s is the extraordinary close correspondence between George Cochran Lambdin's *Among the Roses* (1877; cat. 42) and an undated painting, *The Coquette* (cat. 43) bearing the signature of New York City painter John George Brown (1831–1913). If the paintings are based on a shared photograph rather than on another point of connection—a copy, a forgery, or misattribution—then the photograph would probably have been made in the 1870s, as is deduced from the style of the fresh white cotton frock worn by the young maiden, whose spotless starched clothing and white stockings suggest that she is "dressed up" for a warm summer afternoon.[44]

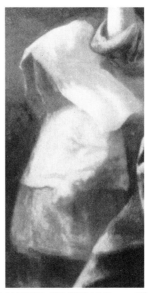

Fig. 9 THE AMATEUR CIRCUS (1869; cat. 16), detail
Courtesy of the North Carolina Museum of Art, Raleigh

Even Lambdin's floral studies—or at least the inspiration for painting out of doors against a wall or solid background—may have been derived from photographs. The flower studies made in the 1850s by European photographer Adolphe Braun (1811–1877) had been distributed and displayed in Philadelphia and New York as early as 1868; Lambdin would have had numerous opportunities to see them in both cities.[45] Certainly there is a remarkable similarity in conception between Lambdin's "Ruskinian" rose studies and Braun's photographs, one of which is illustrated in figure 7. It seems certain that Lambdin was influenced by both Braun's placement and arrangement of flowers within the picture space and his use of light backgrounds.

Lambdin's figure and genre compositions also possess a quiet stillness, an arranged, ordered quality and balanced juxtaposition of shapes and colors which minimizes the sense of action or narrative. As noted earlier, one critic even referred to a Lambdin genre composition as "still life."[46] This ordered stillness probably reflects Lambdin's reliance on photographic models, which allowed him to arrange his shapes and figures carefully against backgrounds of relatively shallow three-dimensionality. His use of photographs may also explain his frequent repetition of themes and the existence of similar versions of the same subject.

Fig. 8 LITTLE WHITE HEIFER (1876; cat. 34), detail
Courtesy of the Lagakos Turak Gallery, Philadelphia

40

42 AMONG THE ROSES, 1877.
Courtesy of Mr. and Mrs. Robert Austin

43 THE COQUETTE by John George Brown (1831–1913)
Courtesy of Christie, Manson & Woods International

Fig. 10

Fig. 11

Fig. 12

Fig. 13

Fig. 14

Fig. 15

Cat. D (Figs. 10–18) Albumin prints, circa 1862–65, once owned by George C. Lambdin.
Courtesy of the Historical Society of Pennsylvania

Fig. 16

Fig. 17

Fig. 18

43

Professional Activities, Writings, and Artistic Theories

We are deprived of the intimate view of Lambdin which a long series of letters to a close friend or beloved family member might have offered, and, as of yet, no diary, record books, or autobiographical recollections have surfaced. Since Lambdin apparently never married, he left no direct descendents. Only two of his six siblings who reached adulthood are known to have married, although the records are incomplete. Children born to his sister Annie have not yet been traced; and Alfred had only one son, John Oldmixon Lambdin (1873–1923), a Baltimore drama and music critic who died unmarried, and whose will makes no mention of his uncle's or grandfather's paintings or possessions. Thus we must turn to George Cochran Lambdin's family background, the record of his professional associations, the ideas he expressed in his writings, and the insights of art critics who knew him in order to round out the picture of the man and the artist.

George's father, James, was an energetic and creative man, who in 1828, at the age of twenty-one, had established the first museum west of the Allegheny mountains: The Museum of Natural History and Gallery of Paintings in Pittsburgh. The art collection included paintings by Thomas Doughty, Gilbert Stuart, Thomas Sully, and Charles Willson Peale. After moving to Philadelphia, the elder Lambdin became a leading figure in artistic circles. For three decades, beginning shortly after his 1837 arrival in Philadelphia, he held various posts in the Artists' Fund Society, serving as its president from 1845 to 1867. He served as director of the Pennsylvania Academy of the Fine Arts from the mid-forties to the mid-sixties and he also served on its committee on instruction and many times chaired the exhibition committee. In the early 1860s he was a professor of fine arts at the University of Pennsylvania. George Lambdin benefitted from his father's contacts, associations, sources of information, and wide-ranging interests. This seems especially true in his young years, when his early exhibition record must have been fostered by his father and the kindly gestures of his father's colleagues in Philadelphia and other cities. One might say that he was "born with a silver-handled brush in his hand."

George's younger brother, Alfred, received a medical degree from the University of Pennsylvania, but soon abandoned medicine for a literary career. He became editor of the *Germantown Chronicle* in 1870, then editor for the *Philadelphia Times*, and finally editor, art and music critic for the Philadelphia *Public Ledger*. Considered "one of the best-known connoisseurs and authorities in music and art in Philadelphia," he held memberships in the Art Club and Musical Art Club, as well as the Academy of Natural Sciences of Philadelphia.[47] Thus George's immediate family could offer both an entrée to artistic circles and acquaintance with contemporary art critics.

George became active in artistic affairs in the fifties. In 1858 he joined some thirty other Philadelphia artists at the National Convention of Artists in Washington, D.C., where more than a hundred American artists, led by James Lambdin, protested a government commission offered a French artist rather than to an American.[48] During the sixties, he was elected Academician at both The Pennsylvania Academy of the Fine Arts and The National Academy of Design, and as president and member of the Board of Directors of the Artists' Fund Society of Philadelphia.

Lambdin was a founding member of the Germantown Horticultural Society, and its first secretary in 1873–74. While in this office he read (and later published) a short paper on "The Close Pruning of Shade Trees" (cat. F and G). This was not a discussion of gardening methods, but rather a statement of "indignation"—at the "butchering" of "what had been trees, the shapely work of God's hands, with their graceful curving limbs and delicate twinery of branches and twigs, bare against the sky, now withered, their heads chopped off, their limbs severed asunder, nothing left to them but the naked unsightly trunks, with the hideous stumps reminding one of the sights about a hospital the time of the war."[49] The entire speech and article echo his visual sensitivity, his interest in growing things, and his civic pride in Germantown, for he concludes with recommendations for new plantings in his community. In Germantown, George was an active member of the Episcopal congregation of St. Michael's Church, where he served several times as Warden in the 1870s. (And there, between 1860 and 1890, he and his siblings—especially his younger sister Emma Connor Lambdin, who must have been a nurturing and involved member of her community—became Godparents to no less than seventeen children.)[50]

In 1874, George contributed an illustration for the premier volume of the *Philadelphia Sketch Club Portfolio;* on January 28 of the following year, along with a group that included fellow artists William Trost Richards and George W. Pettit, he was honored at a special dinner organized by the Sketch Club.[51]

Lambdin was a sought-after public speaker in the mid-1880s. On May 15, 1885, he lectured at the Pennsylvania Academy on "The Invention of Oil Painting and its Development," (cat. H) and when invited to lecture at the National Academy of Design later that year, chose a similar topic (cat. I). In June of the same year, he gave the annual address to the students at the Pennsylvania School of Industrial Art, ardently suggesting the consolidation of Philadelphia's several art schools into a single institution. Three weeks later he delivered the commencement address to the School of Design for Women, where he was an instructor of flower painting and perspective.[52]

He also gave private lessons; in the 1880s he maintained a classroom across the hall from his studio in the Baker Building. The Baker Building, located on Chestnut Street just above Fifteenth Street, was for Philadelphia artists what the Tenth Street Studio Building had been in New York: separate studios in a shared working place which allowed for fellowship, exchange of ideas, joint exhibitions, and receptions for the public. In the mid-eighties about seventeen artists maintained studios in the Baker Building. The first floor was an exhibition area called "The American Art Parlors." The building also served as headquarters of the Artists' Fund Society. Lambdin's fellow tenants included James B. Sword, Newbold H. Trotter, Prosper L. Senat, Frederick DeBourg Richards, George B. Wright, and F. F. de Crano.[53]

Lambdin's studio, illustrated in figure 19, was a typical late nineteenth-century American artist's studio, filled with an assortment of objects that were pleasing and decorative in their own right—thus enhancing the ambience of the room—in addition to draperies, bric-a-brac, furniture, and other artist's props. In late 1885 a writer described the room:

> This studio is in the upper part of the Baker Building, . . . a room of moderate size, with skylight, and windows looking toward the west . . . [but] curtained and screened off. . . . The walls are papered with common brown paper, over which are hung curtains of dark material reaching from near the ceiling to the floor. On the walls are some groups of barbarous weapons, some copies from Titian, and a few studies from life. There are several beautiful pieces of old furniture, chests of drawers and tables, but the most valuable thing possessed is a high-backed armchair of dark wood, handsomely carved. . . . When the late Mr. William Page was looking about for a chair in which to seat his "Shakspere," he was glad to use this [seventeenth-century] chair of Mr. Lambdin's. . . . Over the fireplace hang some shelves of ebony, on which are . . . some old Chinese and Japanese carvings and some fine pieces of Majolica. Near by stands a beautiful female torso cast from a Greek marble, young and tender, and alongside of it is the inevitable skull, without which no artist's studio can be quite complete.[54]

The seventeenth-century chair appears in *Small Pets* (cat. 12); and the Greek female torso may be the same as that noted in his *Consecration, 1861* (cat. 10). A photograph of George Cochran Lambdin (cat. J) shows him standing in his Baker Building studio with two paintings typical of his work of the eighties.

Lambdin accepted at least one important commission as an interior decorator. In 1885 he redecorated the dining room of the brick-and-brownstone townhouse then belonging to prominent Philadelphian Fairman Rogers (1833–1900). One critic wrote: "Mr. Lambdin originated and executed a scheme of decoration at once simple, beautiful and appropriate, and it is greatly to be hoped that this departure from the formal, conventional, tradesman's line of work may induce other householders to . . . do likewise." As had his father, George Lambdin served frequently on exhibition and hanging committees, more than once at critical times in the history of the New York and Philadelphia academies. In 1875, he was a member of the National Academy of Design's hanging committee, a selection committee torn between favoring present academicians or recognizing younger, more innovative painters.[55]

In the 1885 controversy over unclothed models which reverberated around Thomas Eakins and penetrated Philadelphia's social and cultural circles, Lambdin chose his words carefully.

> . . . The figure which expresses humanity moving in the fairy land of poetry, innocence and youth must always represent the highest ideal of beauty, both in form and color. Any artist familiar with nature and with the ideal figures of the Greek and Italian masters, looks upon the nude figure as the landscape painter regards the mountain forms or the sunset clouds, as the loftiest, noblest thing for him to strive for. . . . Art is not a mere imitation of nature; it is a realization of the conceptions of the soul—in sculpture, by means of the forms; in painting, by means of the forms and colors of the objects in nature. If the artist's imagination rests upon ignoble things his work will be ignoble, no matter what form it may take. If it loves to dwell upon that which is refined and delicate, nowhere can he discover a theme to compare both in form and color with the idealized human figure.[56]

Lambdin's writings reveal an artistic philosophy quite in keeping with his painting—both certainly dwelled upon the "refined and delicate." He believed that "an object is picturesque when it is beautiful," and hastily added that he defined "picturesque" narrowly: "A locomotive has a certain beauty, but it is not picturesque, because its lines are hard, angular and unyielding. The human body is also an engine which is entirely picturesque, and the more so the more perfect it becomes."[57]

Because he chose an artistic career early in life, his formal education was limited; however, like most nineteenth-century gentlemen, he was well versed in literature.[58] He readily quoted from or referred to such authors as Pindar and John Flaxman in his essays and had a propensity for titling paintings with passages from English literature.

The links between Lambdin and Ruskinian thought are further elucidated in the writings of Leslie W. Miller (1848–1931), a leading figure in Philadelphia

INTERIOR OF STUDIO OF GEORGE C. LAMBDIN.

Fig. 19 Interior of Studio of George C. Lambdin, from Anne H. Wharton, "Some Philadelphia Studios," *The Decorator and Furnisher* (December 1885), page 78.
Courtesy of the Henry Francis du Pont Winterthur Museum Library: Collection of Printed Books

51 ANNE SOPHIA PENN CHEW ALSTON, circa 1881
Courtesy of Cliveden, a co-stewardship property of
the National Trust for Historic Preservation

artistic and educational circles and a man who would have known Lambdin well:

> Mr. Lambdin's "Patricia" is one of the most successful pictures in the [February 1884 exhibition of the Philadelphia Artists' Fund Society] and one of the best things he has ever exhibited here. It is a portrait; but it is more than that. It is a very graceful and at the same time a very strong portrayal of a type of beauty whose subtler charms very few painters even attempt to render. Mr. Lambdin is evidently one of those who feel that perfect delicacy does not imply want of strength; and in the exquisite tones of this tender flesh and the soft textures of the sitter's dress one sees to what purpose he has studied the tints of roses until he has become probably the best-known flower painter in America. Mr. Ruskin advises his pupils to paint peaches and plums, if they would learn how to paint the more delicate bloom of cheeks and lips. Mr. Lambdin has gone to the roses for the same lesson, and he has certainly learned it well.[59]

Apparently, George Lambdin pursued his late studies of flowers and women as scientific research, or as one reviewer called it, a search for a "floral scheme of color." He wrote, "Mr. George C. Lambdin is busy at his place in Germantown, in the midst of his roses, as usual at this time of the year, and will be occupied with color studies during this month, in pursuit of his idea that the rose holds the secret of color, to be revealed only to the faithful few who are able and willing to pay a great price to obtain it, the price of unvarying, intelligent research." Later that year, Lambdin is quoted, "See . . . how exactly this picture of the girl, pink, white and flesh color, corresponds with the picture of the roses, every tint and tone in one may be matched with a tint or tone in the other."[60] A similar careful matching of tones is found in his portrait of Anne Sophia Penn Chew (Alston) (cat. 51), in which the warm colors in her bouquet accentuate her skin tones.

Anne Chew was a Philadelphian; but by the mid-1880s Lambdin's considerable reputation as a portraitist was bringing him commissions from other cities. Lamenting Philadelphia's "provincialism" and lack of "metropolitan appreciation" towards the arts, a critic wrote, "George C. Lambdin remains here, it is true, and has won an enviable repute as a painter of lovely young girls and reigning belles, but they are New York and New England beauties, seldom Philadelphians."[61]

In sum, the picture of the painter which emerges from the record of his artistic activity, his writings, and the words of his critics is one of a successful and erudite gentleman, conservative to be sure, but also very seriously intent on pursuing carefully articulated artistic theories and speaking to his personal ideals.

The Final Years

In early January 1887 Lambdin was enlisted to fill a vacancy on the Jury of Selection and Hanging Committee of the 57th Annual Exhibition of the Pennsylvania Academy, and was subsequently elected chairman. This was a landmark committee, at a significant point in the growth of the academy, for the directors had turned the management of the exhibition over to the artists (perhaps to reassure its members after the unfortunate events surrounding Thomas Eakins's resignation the previous year) and the committee, for the first time in history, included women. The Philadelphia press applauded:

> Mr. Lambdin served on the committee for the . . . previous exhibition, and it seemed hardly fair to demand a further contribution of his time and labor on this occasion, but . . . the necessity for action became urgent, and he finally consented to put his shoulder to the wheel once more. He immediately organized the committee, taking the hardest and most thankless part of the work, and the circulars were thereafter issued as promptly as possible.[62]

But this was to be the last time he put his shoulder to the wheel. Only three months later the press announced that he must "relinquish work for a time" because of ill health and within a week, on the evenings on April 6 and 7, 1887, Davis & Harvey's Galleries, 1212 Chestnut Street, Philadelphia, offered approximately one-hundred Lambdin paintings for sale—"the contents of his studio" including older works yet unsold as well as many newer canvases, some unfinished (cat. L). From this extraordinary collection, 85 pieces were sold for a total of $3,343, with some examples of rose still lifes in oil selling for as little as $30 to $75 each.[63] The floral studies were of a wider variety of subjects than his surviving paintings indicate, and included *Golden Rod, Lilacs, Cyclamens, Wild Flowers,* and *A Tulip Bed* in addition to more than 30 rose paintings (in both oil and watercolor). Moreover, there were numerous genre and figure studies, including *Among the Roses, A Child of the Sun,* and *Music and Refreshments,* which are either the same paintings as, or very similar versions of catalogue numbers 42, 31, and 32 in the present exhibition. The Davis & Harvey exhibition must have been spectacular!

The list of paintings in the 1887 sale catalogue is filled with surprises: Although Lambdin had exhibited *Over the Sea* at the Pennsylvania Academy in 1866, *On a Summer Sea* at Chicago and New York City in 1875, and again at the Philadelphia Centennial in 1876, and *Butterfly on the Shore* in Louisville in 1886, we are not prepared for the large number of seascapes which this final exhibition and sale included: *By the Sea, When the Ships Come In, Looking Out to Sea, East Gloucester—Mass., Watching the Boats, Near Gloucester, Mass.,* and *A Glimpse of the Sea* are among those offered for sale. In 1877 *The*

Art Journal had reported that his *The Young Boatbuilders* had been based on sketches made at "Squan" (possibly Manasquan) New Jersey.[64] It appears that in his last years he devoted more time to seascapes and figure studies with a seaside background or theme than has previously been recognized. Yet the whereabouts of these paintings are unknown today.

Following the sale, Lambdin further curtailed his activities. He served on the Committee of Selection for the National Academy of Design's Sixth Autumn Exhibition later that year, and exhibited one painting, *Flowers by a Window* the following year in Philadelphia. (This may be the same painting which the Artists' Fund Society of Philadelphia later published in its gift volume, *A Mosaic* (1891; cat. M), with a poem by Austin Dobson and a short message about the kindliness of placing a "rose-message" in a window). In early 1889, his father died. Only George and Emma remained in Germantown. A handwritten note on a probate petition, dated February 20, 1889, for the will of the elder Lambdin reveals that "George Cochran will not qualify," suggesting that his illness had already become so severely debilitating that he was unable to carry out his duties as an executor. For the next eight years George Cochran Lambdin remained incapacitated and lived at his father's Price Street home. He died on January 28, 1896. Two days later he was buried in St. Luke's churchyard, Germantown, in the presence of a delegation of artists, led by his colleague and family friend John Sartain. A laurel wreath containing a cluster of "the roses the artist had loved so well"—sent by the Artists' Fund Society—was placed upon the coffin.[65]

George Cochran Lambdin's work evinces an unusually broad range of subject matter that was painted over a period of thirty years without notable changes in style or technique—except that the floral studies of the seventies show a sophistication and technical proficiency presaged by certain early works but not apparent in all of them. In choosing such a wide range of subjects, Lambdin reflected both the artistic trends and the intellectual influences of his time. He approached his subjects with an attitude of respect—even sentimentality—regarding the separate world of children; the dignity of women; the pain of absence and forebearance in wartime; the exquisite construction, textures, and colors of flowers; and the bloom of youth in relation to the delicacy of flowers. We can easily imagine that Lambdin approached his floral studies intending that they should elicit the same exquisitely delicate emotional response as did the poignant *Our Sweetest Songs* or the almost maudlin *The Last Sleep*. We whose senses have been jarred and intellects challenged by the blatant but cryptic messages of Abstract Expressionism, Computer Art, Op Art and Pop Art, must learn to see George Cochran Lambdin's works as did critic Paul Mantz at the 1867 Paris exposition. Mantz asked, "Is Mr. Lambdin a good painter?" He then promptly settled the matter, "I do not know; but he is 'un *sensitif* of an exquisite sort.'"[66]

45 ROSES IN A WHEELBARROW, n.d. *Courtesy of the Moore Collection; R.H. Love Galleries, Inc.*

NOTES

Information about works exhibited in the nineteenth century has not been given in footnotes if that information has come from standard sources: e.g., Anna Wells Rutledge, Ed., *Cumulative Record of Exhibition Catalogues, The Pennsylvania Academy of the Fine Arts, 1807–1870, The Society of Artists, 1800–1814, The Artists' Fund Society, 1835–1845*. American Philosophical Society Memoir no. 38. (Philadelphia, 1955) or Maria Naylor, Ed., *The National Academy of Design Exhibition Record, 1861–1900*, 2 vols. (New York: Kennedy Galleries, 1973); or the computerized Pre-1877 *Art Exhibition Catalogue Index, National Museum of American Art*.

[1] Paul Mantz, "Les Beaux-Arts a l'Exposition Universelle. X. Etats-Unis," *Gazette des Beaux-Arts*, 23 (1867): 229.

[2] For recent research see William H. Gerdts, *Down Garden Paths: The Floral Environment in American Art* (Cranbury, N.J.: Fairleigh Dickinson University Press, 1983) passim; William H. Gerdts, *Painters of the Humble Truth* (Columbia: University of Missouri Press, 1981) passim; William H. Gerdts and Russell Burke, *American Still-Life Painting* (New York: Praeger, 1971) passim; Ella M. Foshay, *Reflections of Nature: Flowers in American Art* (New York: Alfred A. Knopf, 1984) passim; and John Wilmerding, "The American Object: Still-Life Paintings," *An American Perspective: Nineteenth-Century Art from the Collection of Jo Ann and Julian Ganz* (Washington, D.C.: National Gallery of Art, 1981), pp. 92–103, 149–150. For the genre works, see Patricia Hills, *The Painters' America* (New York: Praeger, 1974), pp. 65, 68–9; and Hermann Warner Williams, Jr. *The Civil War: The Artists' Record* (Boston: Beacon Press, 1961). Nos. 13, 57. Nineteenth-century accounts are Clara Erskine Clement and Laurence Hutton, *Artists of the Nineteenth Century and Their Works* (Boston: Houghton, Osgood, 1879), p. 32; Henry T. Tuckerman, *Book of the Artists; American Artist Life* (1867; reprint New York: James F. Carr, 1967), pp. 450–51; and Anne H. Wharton, "Some Philadelphia Studios: First Paper," *Decorator and Furnisher* 7 (December 1885): 78.

[3] For James Lambdin, see J. O'Connor, Jr., "Reviving a Forgotten Artist: A Sketch of James Reid Lambdin, The Pittsburgh Painter of American Statesmen," *Carnegie Magazine* 12 (September 1938): 115–18. Alfred C. Lambdin to J. D. Woodward, [1892], advises the Academy that the correct spelling of James Lambdin's middle name is "Read" (Pennsylvania Academy of the Fine Arts archives).

[4] This information has been deduced from several sources: U.S. Census Records, 1850, Germantown, Philadelphia Co., Pa., p. 255 (microfilm); obituaries of several family members; burial records at the Germantown Historical Society; manuscript records at Christ Church and Saint Michael's, Germantown; gravestones, Saint Luke's churchyard, Germantown; and James R. Lambdin, "Journal," typescript (MG6, Division of Archives and Manuscripts, Pennsylvania Historical and Museum Commission).

[5] S[amuel] Austin Allibone to George Lambdin, June 5, 1854, asks him to take care of various matters abroad, mentions Italy, France, and London, and wishes him "much pleasure" on the trip (Historical Society of Pennsylvania). Clement and Hutton, *Artists*, p. 32, date his European trip from 1855 to 1857 and say he studied "chiefly in Munich and Paris." (p. 32). Wharton, "Some Philadelphia Studios," (p. 78), apparently based on an interview gives no dates but states that he "studied in Munich, Paris, and Rome." Lambdin is not listed in H. Barbara Weinberg, "Nineteenth-Century American Painters at the École des Beaux-Arts," *American Art Journal* 13 (Autumn 1981): 66–84. "Sketchings," *Crayon* 1 (February 7, 1855): 92; "Sketchings," *Crayon* 1 (May 16, 1855): 314. An anonymous gift to its present owner from a curator of American art, *Girl in a Lavender Dress*, bears a notation on the cardboard backing: "Geo. C. Lambdin?/painted in Dusseldorf?" (Information from Marion L. Grayson, Curator, Museum of Fine Arts, St. Petersburg, 1982). "Sketchings," *Crayon* 3 (December 1856): 375–76.

[6] G. C. Lambdin gave all 4 lines as the title when it was exhibited at the Pennsylvania Academy in 1855.

[7] "Sketchings," *Crayon* 4 (July 1857): 223.

[8] I am greatly indebted to Professor Karin Calvert, Department of American Civilization, University of Pennsylvania, for this and all other information pertaining to costume, social attitudes towards dress, and related considerations in this publication.

[9] William B. Becker, "The American *Cliché Verre*," *History of Photography* 3 (January 1979): 72. *Cliché verre* is described in an advance notice for *Autograph Etchings* published in *Crayon* 6 (September 1859): 289: "The process is that of etching on plates of glass, prepared according to photograp[h]ic principles, from which any number of impressions can be printed. The superiority of the process to that of the old process of etching on copper or steel, is that *any* artist, with a common needle, is able to etch his design upon the glass, without that previous practice with the dry point and skill in laying grounds that are required for etching on metals. The new process may not furnish all the delicate resources of the old process, but it is sufficiently expressive to enable amateurs to enjoy the *thought, style* and *touch* of the artist in a more complete and perfect form than ordinarily within our reach."

[10] "National Academy of Design: Second Notice," *Crayon* 7 (June 1860): 172.

[11] Information from the Pennsylvania Academy Archives, kindly provided by Catherine Stover, Archivist (1982) and Cheryl Leibold, Archivist (1986).

[12] A recent art exhibit devoted to the subject of paintings of nineteenth-century American family life is Lee M. Edwards, *Domestic Bliss* (Yonkers, N.Y.: Hudson River Museum, 1986).

[13] See the discussion in R. W. B. Lewis, *The American Adam* (Chicago: University of Chicago Press, 1955), p. 26; Kenneth Walter Cameron, *Literary Comment in American Renaissance Newspapers* (Hartford, Ct.: Transcendental Books, 1977), p. 4.

[14] *Reading Party* and *Recruiting Party* are illustrated in *Kennedy Quarterly* 5 (August 1965): 303, No. 336; and *Kennedy Quarterly* 15 (January 1977): 68, No. 47. A version of *The New Knife* is illustrated in *Antiques* 109 (May 1976): 923. This painting, which measures 16 × 12 inches, may not be the same as that listed in the Artists' Fund Society's December 18, 1866, sale catalogue (page 5, No. 20); that painting measured 10 × 13 inches.

[15] For his contribution to the Philadelphia fair, see *Catalogue of Paintings, Drawings, Statuary, Etc., of the Art Department in the Great Central Fair* (2d ed., Philadelphia, 1864), 726, 761, 99; "Cushman Album," *Our Daily Fare* 13 (September 11, 1865): 102.

[16] S. S. Conant, "Fine Arts," *Putnam's Magazine* n.s. 1 (March 1868): 388. The painting was titled *The Anxious Mother*.

[17] I am grateful to Gerald Dobbs, Smithsonian Institution, for confirming my findings regarding the lack of military records for George Lambdin. For James Harrison Lambdin, see 121st Regiment Pennsylvania Volunteers Survivors' Association, *History of the 121st Regiment Pennsylvania Volunteers* (Philadelphia: Burk & McFetridge, 1893) p. 144-45. Brig. Gen. James C. Rice, to G. C. Lambdin, September 18, 1863, Historical Society of Pennsylvania; U.S. Government, Surgeon's General's Office, June 25, 1864, National Archives and Record Administration (I thank Gerald Dobbs for locating this document).

[18] I am grateful to this painting's present owners for making it available for study. There is a possibility that the date reads "1884," although according to Kenneth Lux, the painting, before restoration, was inscribed "Feb. 1866."

[19] Information provided by Gerald Dobbs; "Philadelphia Art Notes," *Round Table* (March 26, 1864): 234, and *Round Table* (September 30, 1865): 60.

[20] Mantz, "Beaux-Arts," p. 229. This is the only American painting Mantz discussed in detail.

[21] "Pennsylvania Academy of the Fine Arts," *Crayon* 5 (June 1858): 179. The painting was also reviewed when in New York the following year: "National Academy of Design: Second Notice," *Crayon* 6 (June 1859): 192.

[22] Tuckerman, *Book of the Artists*, 450-51.

[23] Sigmund Spaeth, *Weep Some More, My Lady* (1927; reprint, New York: Da Capo, 1980), p. 26.

[24] "Chatterton," *National Magazine* 1 (1856), p. 33; Beaumont Newhall, *The History of Photography* (New York: Museum of Modern Art, 1964), p. 60. Lambdin painted one other version of a dead woman, entitled *Woman on Her Deathbed* and dated ca. 1887 when it was listed in Sotheby Parke Bernet's catalogue of November 17-19, 1977, No. 494. This painting shows a mourning woman and a child with the deceased.

[25] George C. Lambdin to [John Ferguson] Weir, December 27, 1867, Archives of American Art (Microfilm 529) (I am grateful to Annette Blaugrund—and by extension to Betsy Fahlman—for bringing this letter to my attention). J. F. Weir to Lambdin, May 19, 1868, Historical Society of Pennsylvania. Annette Blaugrund has published preliminary research for a forthcoming dissertation as "The Tenth Street Studio Building: A Roster, 1857-1895," *American Art Journal* 14 (Spring 1982): 64-71.

[26] S. S. Conant, "Fine Arts: The Winter Exhibition," *Putnam's Magazine* n.s. 3 (January 1869): 122.

[27] Henry David Thoreau, *Journal*, July 16, 1851; "National Academy of Design," *Appleton's Journal* 1 (June 5, 1869): 308.

[28] *Biddle Children* is illustrated in Lois Marie Fink and Joshua C. Taylor, *Academy: The Academic Tradition in American Art* (Washington, D.C.: Smithsonian Institution Press, 1975), p. 174, no. 61.

[29] 121st Regiment Pennsylvania Volunteers, *History*, p. 145. Blaugrund, "Tenth Street Studio," p. 69, lists Lambdin there in 1868-1871, but it seems doubtful that he returned to continuous residence following his trip to Europe and brother's death in 1870.

[30] Weir to Lambdin, May 19, 1868. Stating his wish to reoccupy his studio, Weir hoped not to "inconvenience [Lambdin] or La Farge."

[31] C. P. Hayes, "New Roses," *Horticulturist* 29 (January 1874): 3-5; (February 1874): 39-40. See also "Rose Articles," *Horticulturist* 29 (January 1874): 23, Herbert Welsh, "The Artists of Germantown," *Germantown Site and Relic Society Historical Address No. 9.* (Germantown, 1913), p. 243; and Edwin C. Jellett, "Germantown Gardens and Gardeners," *Germantown Site and Relic Society Historical Address No. 10* (Germantown, 1914), p. 297 and passim. In 1889, William Cochrane witnessed James R. Lambdin's will.

[32] George Cochran Lambdin, "The Charm of the Rose," *Art Union Magazine* 1 (June-July 1884): 137; William Gerdts republished the essay in *Painters of the Humble Truth*, p. 125, and Natalie Spassky has more recently reproduced a part of the essay in *American Paintings in the Metropolitan Museum of Art, Vol. 2: A Catalogue of Works by Artists Born between 1816 and 1845* (New York, 1985), pp. 318-19.

[33] I am indebted to Henry Adams, Samuel Sosland Curator of American Art, Nelson-Atkins Museum of Art, for this observation.

[34] "Flowers and Fruit from Nature," *Prospectus of the Philadelphia School of Design for Women with a Catalogue of Art Studies.* (Philadelphia, 1870), p. 29.

[35] For a study of the chromolithograph in America, see Katharine Morrison McClinton, *The Chromolithographs of Louis Prang* (New York: Clarkson N. Potter, 1973); and Peter C. Marzio, *The Democratic Art* (Boston: David R. Godine, 1979).

[36] Matilda Joslyn Gage, "Woman a Mystery," *Appleton's Journal* 15 (April 29, 1876): 566.

[37] "Art Notes," *American* 11 (February 27, 1886): 300. Lambdin had been working on a similar painting in early 1884. See "Art Notes," *American* 7 (January 5, 1884): 203.

[38] John Ruskin, "Notes on Some of the Principal Pictures Exhibited in the Rooms of the Royal Academy, No. 3, 1857," *The Works of John Ruskin*, E. T. Cook and Alexander Wedderburn (London: G. Allen, 1904), 14:115-16. For the influence of Ruskin in America, see Linda S. Ferber and William H. Gerdts, *The New Path* (Brooklyn, N.Y.: Brooklyn Museum, 1985; Roger B. Stein, *John Ruskin and Aesthetic Thought In America, 1840-1900* (Cambridge, Mass.: Harvard University Press, 1967); David H. Dickason, *The Daring Young Men* (Bloomington: Indiana University Press, 1953); and William H. Gerdts, "The Influence of Ruskin and Pre-Raphaelitism on American Still-Life Painting," *American Art Journal* 2 (Fall 1969): 80-97.

[39] Harrison S. Morris, *Masterpieces of the Sea: William Trost Richards* (Philadelphia: J. B. Lippincott, 1912), especially pp. 10-11; Ferber and Gerdts, *The New Path*, pp. 214-27.

[40] "Lionel," "The Artists' Fund Society, Fourth Annual Exhibition," *New Path* 1 (December 1863), 97.

[41] These albumin prints were found together in a packet labeled (perhaps in G. C. Lambdin's hand): "Price St., Germantown Photographs" and (in another hand?): "These photographs were made of the Lambdin family about 1863–5." In 1914 these were presented to the Historical Society of Pennsylvania by Joseph Jackson, a local historian who worked as an editor for the *Public Ledger* and thus would have known Alfred Lambdin well. (The photographic study for *The Vineyard* is not illustrated herein.) Kenneth Finkel, Curator of Prints, Library Company of Philadelphia, has kindly provided much information about photographs and the activities of photographers in nineteenth-century Philadelphia.

[42] W[illiam] H[olbrook] Beard, to Mr. Lambden, June 5, 1862, Dreer Collection, Historical Society of Pennsylvania. Van Deren Coke, "Camera and Canvas," *Art in America* 49, 1961, p. 69; and Coke, *The Painter and the Photograph* (Albuquerque, N.M.: University of New Mexico Press, 1972), p. 33. An illustration of *Young Girl with a Cat* is in Sotheby Parke Bernet, *Americana*, Sale No. 3981 (April 27, 29, and 30, 1977), lot 466.

[43] John C. Browne, *History of the Photographic Society of Philadelphia* (Philadelphia, 1884) p. 35; for examples from the Rossetti/Morris series see Graham Ovenden, *Pre-Raphaelite Photography* (London: Academy Editions, 1972), frontispiece and pp. 21–41, passim; and Michael Bartram, *The Pre-Raphaelite Camera* (Boston: Little, Brown, 1985), pp. 135–138.

[44] According to Professor Calvert, white stockings indicate that the young woman is dressed for a special occasion. (Dark stockings were worn for every-day attire.) White was both a popular choice for young maidens and a status symbol. The labor involved in the washing, starching, and ironing of summer cottons and linens was considerable. White fabrics suggested affluence and implied one was able to afford servants.

[45] H. Vogel, "German Correspondence," *Philadelphia Photographer* 5 (February 1868): 54–55; "The Exhibition," *Philadelphia Photographer* 6 (July 1869), 218.

[46] "National Academy of Design" *Appleton's Journal* 1 (June 5, 1869): 308.

[47] "Sudden Death of Dr. Lambdin," *Public Ledger* (November 8, 1911), p. 10; "Elections During 1876: Members," *Proceedings of the Academy of Natural Sciences of Philadelphia* (Philadelphia, 1876), p. 399.

[48] *Proceedings of the National Convention of Artists*. (Washington, 1858).

[49] Geo. C. Lambden {i.e., Lambdin}, "On the Close Pruning of Shade Trees," *Gardener's Monthly* 16 (January 1874): 6.

[50] Manuscript records, Christ Church and St. Michael's, Germantown, Pa.

[51] Sidney C. Lomas, "A History of the Philadelphia Sketch Club," vol. 1, 1860–1900, pp. 73–74. The print was published in Philadelphia *Sketch Club Portfolio* 1 (July 1874), as pl. 34: "Rusticus." Information kindly provided by Morris Goldsmith, Sketch Club archivist.

[52] "Art Notes," *American* 10 (June 6, 1885): 7 and "Notes," *American* 10 (June 27, 1885): 125.

[53] "Notes," *American* 7 (October 20 and November 24, 1883): 26, 104; "Art Notes," *American* 8 (May 31 and September 6, 1884): 125, 349.

[54] Wharton, "Some Philadelphia Studios," 78.

[55] "Art Notes," *American* 10 (August 29, 1885): 266–67. The house, which later became the home of Mary Cassatt's brother Alexander, was demolished in 1972 (Richard J. Webster, *Philadelphia Preserved* {Philadelphia: Temple University Press, 1976}, pp. 142–43). Fink and Taylor, *Academy*, 75–77.

[56] Geo. C. Lambdin, "An Artist's View of the Nude Question," *American* 10 (July 4, 1885): 141.

[57] Geo. C. Lambdin, "The Picturesque," *American* 11 (February 27, 1886): 301.

[58] One source mentions that on his arrival in Philadelphia, he "[went] to school to Dr. Faires." See obituary, "G. C. Lambdin Dead," *Public Ledger*, (January 29, 1896), p. 2.

[59] L[eslie] W. M[iller], "The Artists' Exhibition: Second Notice," *American* 7 (February 9, 1884): 281.

[60] "Notes," *American* 10 (June 13, 1885), 91. Wharton, "Some Philadelphia Studios," 78.

[61] "Art Notes," *American* 11 (January 30, 1886): 237.

[62] "Art Notes," *American* 13 (January 15, 1887): 204. See also January 7, 1887, Minutes, Committee on Exhibitions, 1880–1887, Pennsylvania Academy of the Fine Arts (Academy Archives).

[63] "Art Notes," *American* 13 (April 2 and April 9, 1887): 382, 398. By this time the public taste for "Lambdin's roses" may have diminished, for the second report suggests that prices were cheap.

[64] D. C. M., "Spring Exhibition at the Philadelphia Academy of Arts," *Art Journal*, n.s. 3 (1877): 190.

[65] "Geo. C. Lambdin Dead," *Germantown Guide* (February 1, 1896), p. 2.

[66] Mantz, "Beaux-Arts," p. 229. Mantz called Lambdin "un *sensitif* d'un ordre exquis." In this play on words, he is likening Lambdin to an exotic variety of Sensitive Plant.

38 STILL LIFE, 1876
  Courtesy of the Collection of Mr. and Mrs. Charles Shoemaker, and Charles B. Tyler,
  Los Angeles, and Richard York Gallery, New York

CATALOGUE OF THE EXHIBITION

1 GIRL IN A LAVENDER DRESS, n.d.
Oil on textured paper on cardboard, 6¹/₄ × 5³/₈ inches
(15.9 × 13.6 cm.)
Lent by the Museum of Fine Arts, St. Petersburg,
Florida
(Illus., p. 7)

2 GIRLS AND FLOWERS, 1855
Oil on canvas, 22¹/₈ × 18¹/₈ inches (56.1 × 45.9 cm.)
Lent by the National Museum of American Art,
Smithsonian Institution
(Illus., p. 36)

3 CLASPING A BRACELET, 1857
Oil on canvas, 26 × 22 inches (66.1 × 55.9 cm.)
Lent by the Kennedy Galleries, New York
(Illus., p. 11)

4 LEARNING THE ALPHABET, n.d.
Oil on canvas, 32 × 38 inches (81 × 97 cm.)
Lent by Dr. Boyd Myers
(Illus., p. 14)

5 THE BASHFUL MODEL, 1862
Oil on panel, 9¹/₂ × 11¹/₂ inches (24.2 × 29.2 cm.)
Lent anonymously
(Illus., p. 15)

6 SITTING IN THE SUN, GERMANTOWN, 1862
Oil on panel, 9³/₄ × 7¹/₄ inches (24.7 × 18.4 cm.)
Lent by Henry Melville Fuller
(Illus., p. 13)

7 A STOLEN LILY, 1864
Oil on stretched canvas (part of a book to benefit the
Union wounded), 7³/₄ × 5¹/₈ inches (19.7 × 13 cm.)
Lent by M.R. Schweitzer, Schweitzer Gallery,
New York
(Illus., p. 24)

8 WEARY, TIRESOME WINTER QUARTERS—
CULPEPER CO. VA., 1864
Oil on canvas, 14 × 17 inches (35.4 × 43.2 cm.)
Lent anonymously
(Illus., p. 35)

9 ROSY REVERIE, 1865
Oil on canvas, 24 × 20 inches (61 × 50.8 cm.)
Lent by the Board of Governors of the Federal Reserve
System, Washington, D.C.
(Illus., p. 57)

10 THE CONSECRATION 1861, 1865
Oil on canvas, 24 × 18¹/₄ inches (61 × 46.3 cm.)
Lent by the Indianapolis Museum of Art: James E.
Roberts Fund
(Illus., p. 20)

11 WINTER QUARTERS IN VIRGINIA, 1864–5, 1866
Oil on panel, 11 × 14 inches (28 × 35.7 cm.)
Lent by Mr. and Mrs. George C. Woodward

12 SMALL PETS, 1867
Oil on canvas backed by panel, 17 × 13 inches
(43.2 × 33 cm.)
Lent by Mr. and Mrs. Walter Rubin
(Illus., p. 16)

27 CALLA LILIES, 1874. *Courtesy of the Berry-Hill Galleries, New York*

28 CALLA LILIES, 1874. *Courtesy of © Sotheby's, Inc.*

40 PINK AND YELLOW ROSES, 1877

20 ROSES, 1872. *Courtesy of Joseph T. Butler*

9 ROSY REVERIE, 1865
  Courtesy of the Board of Governors of the Federal Reserve System, Washington, D.C.

13 LAZY BONES, 1867
Oil on canvas, 13 × 16 inches (33 × 40.7 cm.)
Lent by Mr. and Mrs. Richard Trotter
(Illus., p. 17)

14 PLAYMATES, 1868
Oil on canvas, 15 × 11³/₄ inches (38 × 31 cm.)
Lent by a private collection; Courtesy R. H. Love
Galleries, Inc.
(Illus., p. 24)

15 THE VINEYARD, n.d.
Oil on canvas 24 × 18 inches (61 × 45.7 cm.)
On temporary loan from The J. M. Smucker Company,
Orrville, Ohio
(Illus., p. 25)

16 THE AMATEUR CIRCUS, 1869
Oil on canvas, 22¹/₄ × 29 inches (56.5 × 74.3 cm.)
Lent by the North Carolina Museum of Art, Raleigh
(Illus., p. 15)

17 WHITE HEIFER CALF, 1869
Oil on canvas backed by panel, 20 × 16 inches
(50.8 × 40.7 cm.)
Lent by the Artemis Gallery
(Illus., p. 26)

18 WILD FRUIT, 1869
Louis Prang chromolithograph (after a painting by
George C. Lambdin), 13 × 9³/₄ inches (33 × 24.8 cm.)
Lent by the Boston Public Library, Print Department

19 A YOUNG GIRL READING, 1872
Oil on canvas, 29¹/₂ × 25 inches (74.9 × 63.5 cm.)
Lent by St. Johnsbury Athenaeum, St. Johnsbury,
Vermont
(Illus., p. 31)

20 ROSES, 1872
Oil on panel, 24 × 14 inches (61 × 35.6 cm.)
Lent by Joseph T. Butler
(Illus., p. 56)

39 STILL LIFE OF ROSES, 1876
Courtesy of Whistler Gallery, Inc.

33 ROSES, 1875
Courtesy of Alan Peusler, Inc., Washington, D.C.

21 ROSES, 1872
   Oil on wood panel, 24 × 11³/₄ inches (61 × 29.9 cm.)
   Lent by the Yale University Art Gallery, Gift of Jo Ann
   and Julian Ganz, Jr.
   (Illus., p. 28)

22 APPLE BLOSSOMS, 1873–74
   Oil on canvas, 16 × 12 inches (40.6 × 30.5 cm.)
   Lent by the Elvehjem Museum of Art, University of
   Wisconsin-Madison, Gift of Mr. and Mrs. Stuart P.
   Feld
   (Illus., p. 62)

23 ROSES ON A WALL, 1874
   Oil on canvas, 20 × 16 inches (50.8 × 40.7 cm.)
   Lent by Mr. and Mrs. William C. Burt

24 THE GOLDEN ROSE, n.d.
   Oil on canvas, 30 × 20 inches (76.2 × 50.8 cm.)
   Lent by Harry and Fern Cohen, New York

25 WHITE LILY (EASTER LILY), 1874
   Louis Prang chromolithograph (after a painting by
   George C. Lambdin), 20 × 13 inches (50.8 × 33 cm.)
   Lent by the Boston Public Library, Print Department

26 Selected progressive proofs of WHITE LILY (from the
   full series totaling thirty-five) by Louis Prang of Boston,
   after a painting by George C. Lambdin.
   Lent by the Hunt Institute for Botanical Documentation,
   Carnegie-Mellon University, Pittsburgh

27 CALLA LILIES, 1874
   Oil on panel, 20 × 11⁷/₈ inches (50.8 × 30.2 cm.)
   Lent by the Berry-Hill Galleries, New York
   (Illus., p. 55)

28 CALLA LILIES, 1874
   Oil on tin, 20 × 14 inches (50.8 × 35.6 cm.)
   Lent by Mr. and Mrs. Richard M. Flynn
   (Illus., p. 55)

29 CALLA LILIES, n.d.
Louis Prang chromolithograph (after a painting by
George C. Lambdin), 20 × 13 inches (50.8 × 33 cm.)
Lent by the Boston Public Library, Print Department

30 PINK AND WHITE ROSES, 1874
Louis Prang chromolithograph (after a painting by
George C. Lambdin) 20 × 13 inches (50.8 × 33 cm.)
Lent by the Boston Public Library, Print Department

31 A CHILD OF THE SUN, 1874
Oil on canvas, 23^1/$_2$ × 19^1/$_2$ inches (59.7 × 49.5 cm.)
Collection of Mr. and Mrs. Jack Marino

32 MUSIC AND REFRESHMENTS, 1875
Oil on canvas, 22 × 29 inches (55.9 × 73.7 cm.)
Lent by the New York State Historical Association,
Cooperstown
(Illus., p. 8)

33 ROSES, 1875
Oil on panel, 20 × 13^7/$_8$ inches (50.8 × 35.3 cm.)
Lent by the Washington County Museum of Fine Arts,
Hagerstown, Maryland
(Illus., p. 59)

34 LITTLE WHITE HEIFER, 1876
Oil on canvas, 20 × 16 inches (50.8 × 40.7 cm.)
Lent by Lagakos Turak Gallery, Philadelphia
(Illus., p. 37)

35 ROSES IN AN ORIENTAL VASE, 1876
Oil on canvas, 20 × 16 inches (50.8 × 40.7 cm.)
Lent anonymously
(Illus., p. 29)

36 ROSES IN AN ORIENTAL VASE, n.d.
Oil on canvas, 20 × 16 inches (50.8 × 40.6 cm.)
Lent anonymously

37 ROSES, 1876
Oil on wood panel, 24 × 12 inches (61 × 30.5 cm.)
Lent by The Arden Collection
(Illus., p. 28)

38 STILL LIFE, 1876
Oil on canvas, 25^1/$_2$ × 20 inches (64.8 × 50.8 cm.)
Collection of Mr. and Mrs. Charles Shoemaker, cour-
tesy of Charles B. Tyler, Los Angeles, and Richard York
Gallery, New York
(Illus., p. 53)

39 STILL LIFE OF ROSES, 1876
Oil on panel, 25 × 13 inches (63.5 × 33 cm.)
Lent by Whistler Gallery, Inc.
(Illus., p. 58)

40 PINK AND YELLOW ROSES, 1877
Oil on canvas, 24 × 14 inches (61 × 35.6 cm.)
Lent anonymously
(Illus., p. 56)

41 ROSES AND WHITE AZALEAS, 1877
Oil on panel, 24 × 11^3/$_4$ inches (61 × 29.9 cm.)
Lent by Frank S. Schwarz & Son, Philadelphia
(Illus., p. 28)

42 AMONG THE ROSES, 1877
Oil on canvas, 20 × 14^1/$_4$ inches (50.8 × 33.6 cm.)
Lent by Mr. and Mrs. Robert Austin
(Illus., p. 41)

43 John George Brown (1831–1913)
THE COQUETTE, n.d.
Oil on canvas, 20 × 16^1/$_4$ inches (51 × 41 cm.)
Lent by Dr. and Mrs. David Edelbaum
(Illus., p. 41)

44 ROSES AND FUCHSIA, 1877
Louis Prang chromolithograph (after a painting by
George C. Lambdin), 21^7/$_8$ × 9^1/$_2$ inches
(55.8 × 24.2 cm.)
Lent by the Boston Public Library, Print Department

45 ROSES IN A WHEELBARROW, n.d.
Oil on canvas, 22^1/$_4$ × 30 inches (56.5 × 76.2 cm.)
Lent by the Moore Collection; Courtesy R. H. Love
Galleries, Inc.
(Illus., p. 49)

53 NEW MOON, TRUE MOON, TRUST I SAY WHO MY TRUE LOVE MUST BE, circa 1885
Courtesy of the George Walter Vincent Smith Art Museum, Springfield, Massachusetts

46 AZALEAS AND ROSES, 1878
Louis Prang chromolithograph (after a painting by
George C. Lambdin), 22 × 9¹/₂ inches
(55.9 × 24.2 cm.)
Lent by the Boston Public Library, Print Department

47 JUNE ROSES, 1879
Oil on canvas, 20 × 14 inches (50.8 × 35.6 cm.)
Lent by John H. Garzoli Fine Art, San Francisco
(Illus., p. 39)

48 AUTUMN SUNSHINE, 1880
Oil on canvas, 30¹/₈ × 20 inches (76.5 × 50.9 cm.)
Lent by the National Museum of American Art,
Smithsonian Institution
(Illus., p. 30)

49 IN THE GREENHOUSE, n.d.
Oil on canvas, 31³/₁₆ × 40 inches (79.2 × 101.7 cm.)
Lent by The Metropolitan Museum of Art, Gift of
Mrs. J. Augustus Barnard
(Illus., p. 33)

50 SPRAY OF ROSES, 1880 or later
Watercolor on stretched paper, 30 × 13 inches
(76.2 × 33 cm.)
Lent by the Chester County Historical Society,
West Chester, Pennsylvania

51 ANNE SOPHIA PENN CHEW ALSTON, circa 1881
Oil on canvas, 45⁵/₈ × 32³/₈ inches (115.9 × 82.2 cm.)
Lent by Cliveden, a co-stewardship property of the
National Trust for Historic Preservation
(Illus., p. 47)

52 Untitled (Spray of Roses), 1884
Oil on canvas, 30 × 20 inches (76.2 × 50.8 cm.)
Lent by Ms. Alexandra Steele

53 NEW MOON, TRUE MOON, TRUST I SAY
WHO MY TRUE LOVE MUST BE, circa 1885
Oil on canvas, 25 × 30 inches (63.5 × 72.2)
Lent by the George Walter Vincent Smith Art
Museum, Springfield, Massachusetts
(Illus., p. 61)

22 APPLE BLOSSOMS, 1873–74
Courtesy of the Elvehjem Museum of Art
University of Wisconsin-Madison, Gift of Mr. and Mrs. Stuart P. Feld

CHECKLIST OF ARCHIVAL MATERIALS

A George C. Lambdin
"Childhood," cliché verre by Lambdin after his painting, *Drawing the Elephant*. Illustration to accompany poem by Thomas William Parsons, in John Whetten Ehninger, *Autograph Etchings by American Artists* (New York: W. A. Townsend, 1859, Plate 8)
Lent by Rare Books Division, Library of Congress

B Unknown artist
Portrait of Captain James Harrison Lambdin, in Survivors' Association, *History of the 121st Regiment Pennsylvania Volunteers* (Philadelphia: Burk & McFetridge, 1893, Plate opposite p. 144)
Lent by the collections of the University of Delaware Library, Newark, Delaware

C Brigadier General James C. Rice
Letter to George C. Lambdin. Army of the Potomac, September 18, 1863
Photograph of original in the collections of the Historical Society of Pennsylvania, Philadelphia

D Unknown photographer or photographers
Group of Albumin prints, taken ca. 1862–1865, and owned by George C. Lambdin
Lent by the Historical Society of Pennsylvania, Philadelphia

E George C. Lambdin
"A Good Day for Sunnies." Photograph by John Moran of a painting by Lambdin, in *Poetic Thoughts, The Artists' Fund Annual: A Collection of Twenty Photographs* (Philadelphia: The Society, 1868, Plate 3)
Lent by Special Collections, Van Pelt Library, University of Pennsylvania

F George C. Lambdin, writing as Secretary, Germantown Horticultural Society
Manuscript notes, September 8, 1873, in "Minutes, January 7, 1873 to November 14, 1876."
Lent by the Germantown Historical Society, Philadelphia

G George C. Lambdin
"On the Close Pruning of Shade Trees," essay in *The Gardener's Monthly and Horticultural Advisor* Vol. 16 (January 1874), pp. 6–7.
Lent by the Library of the Academy of Natural Sciences of Philadelphia

H Pennsylvania Academy of the Fine Arts
Card of invitation to a lecture, "The Invention of Oil Painting and its Development," by George C. Lambdin, May 15, 1885
Lent by the Pennsylvania Academy of the Fine Arts, Philadelphia

I George C. Lambdin
Letter to T. Addison Richards, Secretary, National Academy of Design. Philadelphia, December 5, 1885.
Lent by National Academy of Design, New York

J Unknown photographer
George Cochran Lambdin in his studio
Lent by the Historical Society of Pennsylvania, Philadelphia

K Unknown photographer or photographers
Three group photographs of members of the Artists' Fund Society of Philadelphia, ca. 1886
Lent by the Historical Society of Pennsylvania, Philadelphia

L Davis & Harvey's Galleries. *Catalogue of Valuable Paintings: The Collection of George C. Lambdin . . .* (Philadelphia, 1887)
Lent by the Historical Society of Pennsylvania, Philadelphia

M George C. Lambdin
"Roses at the Window" Photograph of his painting, illustration to accompany poem by Austin Dobson, in Harrison S. Morris, Ed., *A Mosaic by the Artists' Fund Society* (Philadelphia: J. B. Lippincott, 1891, p. 19.)
Lent by Hamilton College Library, Clinton, New York

N Edwin C. Jellett
Photograph of the Lambdin residence at 211 (now 322) Price St., Germantown, in 1902
Lent by the Germantown Historical Society, Philadelphia

Fig. 20 George Cochran Lambdin by an unknown photographer.
Courtesy of The Pennsylvania Academy of the Fine Arts Archives